ROSSETTI

DANTE GABRIEL ROSSETTI

BY

ARTHUR C. BENSON

University Press of the Pacific
Honolulu, Hawaii

Dante Gabriel Rossetti

by
Arthur C. Benson

ISBN: 1-4102-1270-X

Copyright © 2004 by University Press of the Pacific

Reprinted from the 1904 edition

University Press of the Pacific
Honolulu, Hawaii
http://www.universitypressofthepacific.com

All rights reserved, including the right to reproduce this book, or portions thereof, in any form.

In order to make original editions of historical works available to scholars at an economical price, this facsimile of the original edition of 1904 is reproduced from the best available copy and has been digitally enhanced to improve legibility, but the text remains unaltered to retain historical authenticity.

PREFACE

I DESIRE to make grateful acknowledgment to the following for the ready assistance that they have afforded me in a delicate and difficult task. To Mr. W. M. Rossetti first, for his cordial encouragement, as well as his readiness to give information, and for kind permission to make use of his writings on the subject, and detailed assistance with regard to MSS. and pictures; to Mr. Theodore Watts-Dunton for his unfailing kindness, vivid reminiscences, and generous sympathy; to Mr. C. Fairfax Murray, who has given me abundance of information on many points, and has shown a willingness to answer questions and to criticise detailed statements for which I cannot be sufficiently grateful. He also allowed me to make use of his unique collections, and placed at my disposal the large number of Rossetti MSS. which he possesses; to Mr. Hall Caine for his expressed interest, and permission to make use of his memorable *Recollections*; to Mr. Edmund Gosse for patient and invaluable criticism; to Mr. M. H. Spielmann for courteous help and fruitful suggestions; to Mr. Lionel Cust for his willingness to be consulted and his excellent advice; to Dr. Richard Garnett for sound and judicious criticism on Rossetti as a translator; to Mr. J. R. Clayton for interesting information; to Messrs. Ellis and Elvey for permission to quote from the *Collected Works* and other copyright volumes dealing with the subject; to my sister Miss Margaret Benson; to the Hon. Maurice Baring; to Mr. Percy Lubbock for careful and perspicacious criticism; and to Miss Beatrice Layman, for simply invaluable aid in verification and correction.

A. C. B.

AUTHORITIES

THE principal books I have consulted, and to which reference is made in the following pages, beside Rossetti's own publications, are the following :—

The Collected Works of D. G. Rossetti, 2 vols., 1901; *D. G. Rossetti as Designer and Writer*, 1889; *Dante Gabriel Rossetti, Letters and Memoir*, 2 vols., 1895; *Ruskin, Rossetti, Pre-Raphaelitism* (1854-1862), 1899; *Pre-Raphaelite Diaries and Letters* (1835-1856), 1900; *Rossetti Papers*, (1862-1870), 1903; the above all edited or written by *Mr. W. M. Rossetti*.

Letters of D. G. Rossetti to William Allingham (1854-1870), edited by *G. Birkbeck Hill*, 1897; *Recollections of D. G. Rossetti*, by *T. Hall Caine*, 1882; *Dante Gabriel Rossetti*, by *William Sharp*, 1882; *Life of D. G. Rossetti*, by *Joseph Knight*, 1887; *Dante Rossetti and the Pre-Raphaelite Movement*, by *Esther Wood*, 1894; *Dante Gabriel Rossetti*, with illustrations, by *H. C. Marillier*, 1901.

Autobiographical Notes of William Bell Scott, 1892; *Ford Madox Brown*, by *F. M. Hueffer*, 1896; *The Life of William Morris*, by *J. W. Mackail*, 1899.

Essays—Modern, by *F. W. H. Myers*, 1883; *Essays and Studies*, by *A. C. Swinburne*, 1875; *Ward's English Poets*, Introduction to Rossetti's poems, by *Walter Pater*, 1883; *Dictionary of National Biography*, article on *D. G. Rossetti*, by *R. Garnett*, 1897 ; but the list is by no means exhaustive, as there are many contributions to periodical literature such as *The Pre-Raphaelite Brotherhood*, by *W. Holman Hunt*, in the *Contemporary Review*, vol. xlix., 1886 ; and *The Truth about Rossetti*, by *Theodore Watts* (Watts-Dunton) in the *Nineteenth Century*, March 1883, which contain interesting criticism and information not otherwhere given.

A. C. B.

CONTENTS

CHAPTER I
EARLY YEARS 1

CHAPTER II
THE PRE-RAPHAELITES 18

CHAPTER III
LATER LIFE 44

CHAPTER IV
POEMS—CHARACTERISTICS 78

CHAPTER V
POEMS—"HOUSE OF LIFE" 101

CHAPTER VI
TRANSLATIONS—PROSE—LETTERS 145

CHAPTER VII
PAINTING 176

CHAPTER VIII
CHARACTER 202

INDEX 231

ROSSETTI

CHAPTER I

EARLY YEARS

ROSSETTI'S life, it has been well said, has been treated by his biographers too much in the Pre-Raphaelite method: we have been presented with a great mass of detail, highly interesting in itself, but tending somewhat to obscure the distinctness of the central figure. Yet it is hard to see how it could have been otherwise. The seclusion in which in later life Rossetti lived, the fascinated interest which he inspired in those who were admitted within the close-shut doors, the strange light, so to speak, which the initiated brought away glimmering round their brows, from visits to the inmost presence-chamber, the pictures, guarded so jealously from all public displays, the poems, springing from a source of which the secret was so deeply hidden—all these things stimulated public curiosity to an extravagant degree. The result was that a host of distorted legends sprang up round the name of Rossetti, exaggerating all that was morbid, darkening every shadow, dwelling mainly on lapses from conventional standards, and substituting for the brave, genial, robust personality, which the chosen friends still discerned under the overshadowing of doom, an affected, decadent, fantastic figure, posturing in a gloomy *danse macabre*, or wandering in an airless labyrinth of poisonous loveliness.

It was necessary then, at all hazards, for his biographers to tell the truth about Rossetti. But the outcome is that we have been told almost too much of him, and yet not enough. Of the earlier and brighter years the record is comparatively slight. Yet we can follow his footsteps, print by print, along the darkening pilgrimage, while the sombre figure of the dreamer marches heavily along, with sometimes a word and sometimes a glance flashed upon us, but severe, inscrutable, sad with a wilful sadness. With what philosophy he faced the doom that threatened him, how his eager pursuit of the beautiful harmonised, if it did harmonise, with the stubborn insistence of pain and decay, whether he increased in a grim and stoical resistance, or turned his back upon the awful mystery, beguiling the time that still remained to be told; or whether the whole character broadened and deepened under the pressure of the elemental sadness—all this we can never know. And here, I think, lies the deepest tragedy of Rossetti's life. A man of infinite self-will, of intense though limited outlook, sets out upon a certain pilgrimage, with a radiant goal in view, resolutely disregarding all that does not at once accommodate itself to his aims and faiths; and then the vision changes, and he is confronted in the saddest and sternest way with the darkest problems that try and torture the mortal nature. The very gloom of the tragedy lends a deeper augustness to the great figure that slowly moves to meet it. But we may dare to hope that a soul which, though knit with a temperament open in a singular degree to all the nearer seductions of beauty, kept its gaze resolutely on the ultimate hope, the further issue, the central vision, and which looked so earnestly through the symbol to the force symbolised, must attain in some freer region to the knowledge of the secret, that murmured like a phantom music, in divine, mysterious tones round the clouded earthly tabernacle.

Gabriel Charles Dante Rossetti, commonly known as DANTE GABRIEL ROSSETTI, was born on May 12, 1828, at No. 38 Charlotte Street, Portland Place. He was baptized at All Souls Church, Langham Place, according to the rites of the Church of England, his mother being a devoted Anglican, of an Evangelical type in early days, but later holding High Church views. The name Gabriel was his father's name. Charles came from his godfather, Mr. Charles Lyell of Kinnordy, a family friend, a keen student of Italian literature, and father of the celebrated geologist, Sir Charles Lyell. He was called Dante after his father's favourite poet. Rossetti dropped the name Charles in early life; and it is strange that one who never even visited the land of his ancestors, who, as his brother says, "was always ready to reckon to the discredit of foreigners a certain shallow and frothy demonstrativeness," who loved the free country of his nativity so well, should have parted with his only English inheritance. He transposed his other names, that the noble name of Dante might have pre-eminence; and we find him in early manhood writing to his aunt, who addressed him by his legal initials, to ask her to use the nomenclature that he had permanently adopted.

Of his four grandparents, three were pure Italians, one English. His father was Gabriele Rossetti (*b.* 1783), the youngest son of Nicola Rossetti, a blacksmith of Vasto, a town on the Adriatic coast of South Italy. They were simple people: Rossetti's grandmother could neither read nor write.

His mother was Frances Mary Lavinia Polidori, daughter of Gaetano Polidori and his wife Anna Maria (Pierce). Gaetano Polidori was the son of a physician of Bientina, a Tuscan town. He was at one time secretary to Alfieri, and settling in England in 1789, married Miss Pierce, a governess, and taught Italian.

Gabriele Rossetti was a man of active mind, with strong literary tastes, in early days a skilful draughtsman, and always a beautiful reader and reciter. He was an *improvisatore*, a poet, and in early life librettist to the operatic theatre of San Carlo at Naples, being afterwards a Curator in the Museum of Naples. He was in favour with Murat, King of Naples, and held a secretaryship in the department of public instruction at Rome. The Bourbon king, Ferdinand I., was restored to his kingdom in 1815, and Rossetti, being a noted liberal, was proscribed in 1821 when Ferdinand, with the aid of the Austrians, suppressed constitutional government. He escaped to Malta in 1821, in a British uniform, on a man-of-war. Eventually, in 1824, he settled in England and married in 1826. He was appointed Professor of Italian in King's College, London, in 1831. His health declined in 1842, and after some years of invalid life he died in 1854, "glad to be released."

EARLY YEARS

The elder Rossetti was a sensitive, lively, active-minded man, sociable, good-humoured, and affectionate. He was a fervent patriot, and had a high standard of virtue. In religion he was a free-thinker, but with a strongly spiritual nature. He wrote voluminously, patriotic and religious poems, learned treatises, mystical commentaries. His memory, as an enthusiastic ex-patriot and a distinguished man of letters, is greatly revered in Italy. The centenary of his birth was celebrated at Vasto in 1883, and the central piazza of the town renamed after him.

There is a delightful picture of him by his son, drawn in 1853, which represents him sitting at a table, in a cap and dressing-gown, closely scanning a manuscript which throws an upward light on the brow. His white hair grows thickly; the long, thin nose, the compressed lips, the tired but penetrating eyes, all show the man of high enthusiasm, intense intellectuality, and refined character. It is not fanciful to see a certain strain of asceticism and unworldliness in the face, combined with the gentle submission that comes of a faith in ideas and principles lying behind the material world.

There was, it seems, a "certain tinge of self-opinion or self-applause in his temperament"; he liked, said his son Dante, "to ride the high horse." But he was quite without personal vanity, full of kindness, and generously appreciative of the merits of others.

Rossetti's mother was a cultivated woman, fond of reading, characterised by great simplicity of nature; self-controlled, just, kind, abhorring gossip, strongly religious, and entirely devoted to her husband and children. She said once, in 1872, "I always had a passion for intellect, and my wish was that my husband should be distinguished for intellect, and my children too. I have had my wish; and I now wish that there was a little less intellect in the family, so as to allow for a little more common-sense." She had herself no lack of the latter quality. They lived simply enough, and for ten years, when Gabriele Rossetti was disabled by illness, she took pupils, and worked hard for the support of the household. She was, too, an excellent woman of business, and they always lived within their means.

Rossetti's brothers and sisters were three in number: Maria Francesca (1827-1876), who became a member of an Anglican sisterhood; William Michael (b. 1829), who still survives, his brother's careful and accomplished biographer; and Christina (1830-1894), the illustrious poetess. They were thus a family of marked characteristics, with strong literary and artistic gifts, with which was combined, in the sisters, a deep and mystical religion. The early years of the children were passed almost wholly in London. The household had few English acquaintances, but Mr. W. M. Rossetti says that "it seems hardly an exaggeration to say that every Italian staying in or passing through London, of a Liberal mode of political opinion, sought out my father, to make or renew acquaintance with him." There was also a perpetual flow of foreigners requiring assistance, and if a Masonic signal was given, as was often the case, Gabriele Rossetti being a Freemason, they were immediately relieved. Italian patriots, artists, literary men, musicians, vendors of plaster-casts, dancing-masters, eclectics of every kind congregated there, among whom the most famous were Paganini the violinist, and occasionally Mazzini.

The children spoke Italian in the house, and listened to perpetual declamatory political talk, idealistic aspirations, recitations of poetry, and reminiscences of Italy.

It is interesting to note that this seems to have developed in D. G. Rossetti an extreme hatred of politics. It is often to be remarked, in men of strong individuality, that the influences of early life seem to have had a curiously antagonistic effect upon their tastes and character; and the result of this animated political society seems to have confirmed the young poet in a deeply rooted dislike of the lesser or practical politics. "He heard so much," it is said, "in his youth, of *gli Austriaci* (the Austrians) and *Luigi Filippo* (Louis Philippe), that he seems to have registered a vow to leave Luigi Filippo and the other potentates of Europe and their ministers to take care of themselves." For political ideals and principles he seems to have had a faint sympathy, but for practical politics he had what can only be called an aversion, almost amounting to detestation.

A similar influence can be detected in the boy's literary tastes. Gabriele Rossetti was an ardent student of Dante, and fond of abstruse mystical speculations on the subject of the poems. He would sit surrounded with huge folios in ancient type, "about alchemy, freemasonry, Brahminism, Swedenborg, the Cabbala, etc., and filling page after page of prose, in impeccable handwriting full of underscorings, interlineations, and cancellings." Nothing that Dante wrote was allowed to be capable of simple and natural interpretation; every passage and every word was an elaborate vehicle for the concealment of some mystical speculation or political idea, and the highest praise for a book, in Gabriele Rossetti's mouth, was that it was a "libro sommamente mistico."

The result on the children was that though they viewed their father's studies with respect, the books which he loved were understood not to "do to read." But Rossetti re-discovered Dante for himself when he was fifteen or sixteen; and then, relieved of the fear of being obliged to interpret the poems in some remote sense, he mastered them with burning avidity. He wrote in the Preface to *Early Italian Poets*, "In those early days, all around me partook of the influence of the great Florentine; till, from viewing it as a natural element, I also, growing older, was drawn within the circle." But, speaking generally, the studies of their father may be said to have thrown the children, by a species of reaction, rather decidedly into the study of English literature. They read poetry, tales, and wholesome old books, and began very early to try their hand at writing. Neither the early writings nor the early pictures of the child seem to have been markedly promising, but it is interesting that he preferred imaginative designs, such as scenes from Shakespeare, to transcriptions of natural objects, and chose to create rather than copy.

The only one of the early writings which deserves a passing mention, from the fact that it is a bibliographical curiosity, is a poem in four parts called *Sir Hugh the Heron*, which was written at the age of twelve, and printed in 1843 by his grandfather, Mr. Polidori, who had then moved into London, at a private printing-press which he had set up.

An interesting autobiographical reminiscence of his early days occurs in a mystical story, *Saint Agnes of Intercession*, written at a later date. "Among my earliest recollections, none is stronger than that of my father standing before the fire when he came home in the London winter evenings, and singing to us in his sweet, generous tones: sometimes ancient English ditties,—such songs as one might translate from the birds, and the brooks might set to music; sometimes those with which foreign travel had familiarised his youth,—among them the great tunes which have rung the world's changes since '89. I used to sit on the hearthrug, listening to him, and look between his knees into the fire till it burned my face, while the sights swarming up in it seemed changed and changed with the music: till the music and the fire and my heart burned together, and I would take paper and pencil, and try in some childish way to fix the shapes that rose within me. For my hope, even then, was to be a painter."

The boy went in 1836 to a day-school in Portland Place, and to King's College School in 1837, where he stayed till 1842. Here he learned Latin and French well, with a little Greek; German he acquired at home. He had some linguistic aptitude, but held science and mathematics in contempt. He was said to have been a quiet, affectionate boy, courageous, kind, and considerate of others. But his own recollection was different. He described himself to Mr. Hall Caine as having been destitute of personal courage, shrinking from the amusements of his schoolfellows, and fearful of their quarrels, selfish, though not without some generous impulses, and reclusive in habits. The truth probably is that he was intensely preoccupied, like all children of strong individuality, with his own ideas and dreams, and apt to resent anything that diverted the current of them; but he was pre-eminently genial and sociable by nature, and it is impossible that he should not have displayed these qualities to a certain extent when at school. He was always a favourite with simple people, servants, shoe-blacks, organ-grinders, and never had, to the end of his life, the faintest consciousness of or subservience to social position. No doubt the uncongenial atmosphere of school threw him back decidedly upon the circle of home interests. He appears to have made no special friends at school.

In 1841 it was decided that Rossetti had received a sufficient education, and that his professional life had better begin. He was bent on becoming an artist, though it does not appear that up to this date his drawings had shown any special promise. It is interesting that he seems to have been allowed to have his own way in the matter, as the household must have been under the pressure of considerable anxiety owing to the failing health of Gabriele Rossetti. He went first to the drawing academy of Mr. F. S. Cary in Bloomsbury Street. He was there for four years. He appears to have been irregular in attendance, and with moods of brusquerie and unapproachableness, alternating with hilarious gaiety and affectionate generosity. He paid little heed to Cary's instructions, but followed his own methods. "Why were you not here yesterday?" says his instructor, according to the legend. "I had a fit of idleness," says the pupil, and shortly after distributes a sheaf of verses among the students. He said once to his brother, many years after, "As soon as a thing is imposed on me as an obligation, my aptitude for doing it is gone; what I *ought* to do is what I *can't* do." His imagination was, however, strongly stirred by the exhibition of some cartoons in Westminster Hall, prior to the decoration of the Houses of Parliament. Here he first saw the work of Ford Madox Brown, and recognised a new spirit at work, a spirit of originality and fidelity, of revolt against stereotyped traditions. This had an important bearing on his after career. He entered the Antique School of the Royal Academy in 1846, and there is an interesting description of his appearance in those days, given by a fellow-student. "Thick, beautiful, and closely curled masses of rich brown much-neglected hair fell about an ample brow, and almost to the wearer's shoulders; strong eyebrows marked [masked?] with their dark shadows a pair of rather sunken eyes, in which a sort of fire, instinct with what may be called proud cynicism, burned with furtive energy. His rather high cheekbones were the more observable because his cheeks were roseless and hollow enough to indicate the waste of life and midnight oil to which the youth was addicted. Close shaving left bare his very full, not to say sensuous lips, and square-cut masculine chin. Rather below the middle height, and with a slightly rolling gait, Rossetti came forward among his fellows with a jerky step, tossed the falling hair back from his face, and, having both hands in his pockets, faced the student world with an *insouciant* air which savoured of thorough self-reliance. A bare throat, a falling, ill-kept collar, boots not over-familiar with brushes, black and well-worn habiliments, including not the ordinary jacket of the period, but a loose dress-coat which had once been new—these were the outward and visible signs of a mood which cared even less for appearances than the art-student of those days was accustomed to care, which undoubtedly was little enough."

Mr. Holman Hunt says that, on speaking to him, the impression of his insouciance was much modified; "he proved to be courteous, gentle, and winsome, generous in compliment, rich in interest in the pursuits of others, and in every respect . . . a cultivated gentleman."

At this time Rossetti's intellectual ardour was very great. He read Shelley and Keats with profound admiration, and many other poets; in prose he had a taste for the legendary, the strange, the supernatural, combined with a great relish for humorous writing of any kind. He eschewed philosophy, science, history, and politics. In 1847 he discovered Browning, and everything else sank into the background: he revelled in the passion, the dramatic perception, the mediævalism of Browning. He had before this written a prose romance called *Sorrentino*, the MS. of which he afterwards burnt, and had begun to translate the *Nibelungenlied*. He had also taken up Dante and the Italian lyrists and translated everything that pleased him, including Dante's *Vita Nuova*. Some of these translations were shown to Tennyson, who pronounced the work to be strong and earnest, but disfigured by superficial faults. But what is still more striking is that, before entering his twentieth year, he had written *The Blessed Damozel*, in many respects his finest and most characteristic poem; moreover, in the next year or two he wrote the *Ave*, the beginning of *Dante at Verona, The Last Confession, The Bride's Prelude*, and an original draft of *Jenny*, of which the greater part was afterwards cancelled. The whole period gives the impression of intense vitality and strength, but it is even more remarkable to find how early maturity was reached. He seems to have served no patient apprenticeship in literature, but to have come suddenly and swiftly into the possession of his full inheritance.

A good instance of his poetical insight is revealed by the fact that he fell in with an anonymous book at the British Museum called *Pauline*, which he admired sufficiently to copy out; he came to the conclusion that this must be the work of Robert Browning, and wrote to him to ask if it was so. Browning replied in the affirmative, from Venice; but it was not till two years after that the poets met.

In 1848 Rossetti, yielding to impulse in a characteristic way, wrote a remarkable letter to Ford Madox Brown. He said that he had always admired his "glorious" work. "I have always listened with avidity if your name happened to be mentioned, and rushed first of all to your number in the catalogue." The letter goes on to say that Brown's pictures had kept him "standing on the same spot for fabulous lengths of time." He concludes by asking that Madox Brown would accept him as a pupil, as he desired "to obtain some knowledge of colour."

Mr. W. M. Rossetti says that his brother was sick of the slow progress of his artistic education, and desired just to gain sufficient technical knowledge of brush-work to start upon original designs.

Madox Brown was twenty-seven at this date. He

was already working in the spirit of the artistic creed which he afterwards formulated in the two words "emotional truth." Neither then nor later did he receive adequate recognition, though he slowly emerges as one of the most profound and impressive painters of the century. He appears to have been astonished by the letter, and particularly by the lavish praise it contained, as he was by no means accustomed to be so admiringly regarded. He seems to have imagined that some jest was intended, and marched straight to Rossetti's house with a stout stick. Madox Brown was a vigorous-looking man of resolute aspect, with a strongly marked face. He knocked at the door at 50 Charlotte Street,[1] and desired to see Rossetti, but would not come in or give his name. Rossetti came down. "Is your name Rossetti, and is this your writing?" he asked. Rossetti replied that it was. "What do you mean by it?" said Madox Brown, in his distinct and slow articulation. Rossetti explained that he meant what he said, and Madox Brown, seeing that the request was genuine, accepted him on the spot as a pupil and declined to accept, with characteristic indifference to money, any payment. Rossetti went almost immediately afterwards to the studio, and was at once, to his disgust, set down to paint some pickle-jars.

At this date Rossetti made two friends among the Academy students, whose association with him made a great difference in his life. These were Mr. Holman Hunt, about a year older than himself, and John Everett Millais, a year younger. Rossetti had seen Mr. Hunt's picture *The Eve of St. Agnes* in the Academy,

[1] To which house the Rossettis had removed in 1836.

and had said boisterously that it was the best picture of the year. Through Mr. Hunt, Rossetti got to know Millais well, having previously been on terms of mere acquaintanceship with him. Millais had already exhibited several pictures, and was regarded as a paragon of promise. Mr. Hunt advised Rossetti, who had loudly lamented the degrading character of the work he was doing, to begin a large picture, and gain technique by using the still-life objects which he was set to paint as direct pictorial accessories to it. Rossetti eventually chose *The Girlhood of Mary Virgin* as a subject.

But Rossetti was still doubtful at this time as to whether he should definitely take up art or literature. He wrote to Leigh Hunt, to whom he was unknown, sending him some of his poems and translations, and asking his advice. Leigh Hunt replied in a very kindly letter, which is preserved. He seems, like Tennyson, to have been impressed with the roughness of the versification in the translations. "I guess indeed," he wrote, "that you are altogether not so musical as pictorial." But Leigh Hunt expressed himself most generously about the original poems, seeing in them the work of "an unquestionable poet, thoughtful, imaginative, and with rare powers of expression. I hailed you as such at once, without any misgiving." He concludes with some kindly words warning the aspirant against thinking of poetry as a profession. "Poetry," he says, ". . . is not a thing for a man to live upon while he is in the flesh, however immortal it may render him in spirit."

Rossetti joined Mr. Holman Hunt in a studio in Cleveland Street, (now No. 46) Fitzroy Square, a dismal and squalid place, looking out upon a timber-yard, and rendered additionally disagreeable by the fact that a boys' school was kept in the house.

The friendship with Millais was established one night at Millais's house (7 Gower Street), where Millais, the only one of the group whose family was in easy circumstances, worked in a long shed-like studio at the back of the house. There they turned over a book of engravings by Lasinio of the frescoes by early masters in the Campo Santo at Pisa—engravings which Ruskin calls execrable. This was in August 1848, and the incident was to have important consequences.

I cannot but believe that his early *entourage* had a great and lasting effect, both in poetry and art, upon so perceptive a spirit as Rossetti's. In these first years, except for half a dozen visits to the country, to Chalfont and Little Missenden, and a few weeks at Boulogne, he knew nothing of the country pure and simple. He was thus, I think, thrown strongly back into himself, and the desire for beauty driven into one special channel. He has delicate and informing touches of natural observation in his poetry. But so eager an eye for beauty is bound to feed itself upon what it sees, and one can imagine Rossetti, like Leonardo da Vinci, wandering about the streets in search of rare and remote types of human expression. The landscape both of his pictures and poems is rather of the pictorial than of the natural order, imagined ideal places, gardens seen in dreams, with a tender light of evening over lawns and thick-grown trees.

Moreover, the time at which natural impressions sink deepest is when they are studied with the relent-

EARLY YEARS

less, inquisitive gaze, the eager curiosity, the busy hands of childhood. Natural phenomena are not at an early age interpreted or apprehended in the light of beauty, but the harvest is then gathered and the habit acquired; and thus the early London life no doubt accounts for the fact that Rossetti's natural imagery does not rise, as it were, out of a full source, but consists more of little effects noted in some moment of country observation.

There is an interesting fragment of autobiography in the *St. Agnes* which deserves to be quoted here:—

"Any artist or thoughtful man whatsoever, whose life has passed in a large city, can scarcely fail, in course of time, to have some association connecting each spot continually passed and repassed with the labours of his own mind. In the woods and fields every place has its proper spell and mystery, and needs no consecration from thought; but wherever in the daily walk through the thronged and jarring city, the soul has read some knowledge from life, or laboured towards some birth within its own silence, there abides the glory of that hour, and the cloud rests there before an unseen tabernacle."

CHAPTER II

THE PRE-RAPHAELITES

IN the autumn of 1848 the celebrated Pre-Raphaelite brotherhood was constituted. We may trace in this little society, which was destined to have a profound though indirect effect on English art, the dominant mind of Rossetti. He had a mind and a character which, without any assumption of superiority, naturally took the lead in any group of which he was a member, from sheer force of will, absolute knowledge of his own mind, intensity of purpose, and a kind of royal generosity which recognised ungrudgingly and proclaimed unhesitatingly the merits of others. The combination was irresistible: few men can resist the dominion of will, intellectual force allied with noble sympathy.

The name was not a new one. In 1810 two German painters, Cornelius and Overbeck, had founded a society in Rome, called the German Pre-Raphaelite Brethren. The basis of this institution seems to have been rather religious than artistic, and was a protest against the prevailing irreligion of the art and artists of the day. The members practised a species of monastic seclusion, and arrayed themselves in a religious garb of cassocks with rope-girdles. By this

THE PRE-RAPHAELITES

school the name Pre-Raphaelite was chosen because the earlier Italian painters were mostly of a monastic type and consecrated their art to the decoration of sacred buildings.

There was no such idea in the minds of our English Pre-Raphaelites. The genesis of the name appears in a letter written in August 1848, by Rossetti, to his brother William. He says that he has been reading Lord Houghton's *Life and Letters of Keats*, then just published. "He [Keats] seems to have been a glorious fellow, and says in one place (to my great delight) that, having just looked over a folio of the first and second schools of Italian painting, he has come to the conclusion that the early men surpassed even Raphael himself!"

The central idea of the Pre-Raphaelite movement was a revolt against conventionality. The Pre-Raphaelites thought that the English school of painters had fallen into a thoroughly insincere manner. They felt that the English *genre* school, originated by Hogarth, whom they valued for his hard observation and firm naturalism, had degenerated in the hands of Wilkie, Leslie, and Mulready—kindly, childlike masters—into a school of painting characterised by conventional optimism and trivial humour, whose works appealed to the heart rather than to the mind and eye. The Pre-Raphaelites contemned the feeble device of "anecdotal," familiar or melodramatic subjects. They believed that English painters valued little but pretentious, theatrical, and elementary effects, and traded with cheap emotions, false pathos, sentimental ideas. They saw no fundamental conception, no poetical imagination, no faithful delineation. In the designs of Blake alone, whom they were almost the first to appreciate at his true worth, they discerned a poetical imagination and an independent spirit at work. They even contemned the great English portrait-painters. Even Reynolds did not escape, being called "Sloshua" by Millais, a name suggested by the adjective "sloshy," which they applied freely to all indefinite, feeble, and superficial work. They felt that the disadvantage of the appearance of a painter like Raphael, with the inimitable perfection of technique and tranquil sublimity of conception, was that he had influenced too deeply the art of his successors, and tended to destroy originality of design. They maintained that artists ought to paint things as they saw them, and not as they thought Raphael would have seen them. They did not take the earlier painters as a model, but they wished to revert to the principles of an artistic age when a strong and dominating tradition was not at work, but when painters developed art on their own lines with sturdy fidelity, masculine individuality, and serious intention. In these early masters, from Giotto to Leonardo—for they had no great knowledge of Flemish or German schools—they saw an unspoiled delight in art, a genuine devotion, a loving labour which, besides a stirring spiritual intention, had a homely veracity of presentment. In one sense these ancient painters were conventional, but it was only a conventionality of technique, not of conception, and did not override the original impulse of the artist. It was, in fact, a time of enthusiastic development, of workers not hampered with the consciousness of an overpowering treasure of unsurpassable production.

The Pre-Raphaelites did not propose to confine themselves to realistic subjects. In the mediæval pictures, for instance, of Rossetti, there is no antiquarian attempt to reproduce exactly the surroundings that must have figured in the original scene. The convention which mediævalises the scenes of the Gospel story they accepted without question. But they set themselves rather to conceive a subject in a serious and lofty way, and then to see that the details were presented with a strict and austere veracity. But this elaboration of detail was not an essential part of the principles of the Brotherhood. Mr. Holman Hunt says that it was undertaken principally with the idea of arriving at a perfection of technique. "We should never have admitted that the relinquishment of this habit of work by a matured painter would make him less of a Pre-Raphaelite."

In technique, the Pre-Raphaelites began with a clean canvas, and built up their pictures bit by bit, like a mosaic, finishing, as far as might be, each piece of the work, without retouching, before another was begun. But Rossetti did not adhere strictly to this system, except perhaps in one or two of his earliest productions. The Brotherhood used primary colours, and avoided low tones and dark backgrounds, which were at that time the fashion; and instead of aiming at harmony by concentrating colour and working away from a point, they developed each individual portion with the same fidelity. The mistake was that colours do not, in a scene as it appears to the eye, stand alone, but are modified by the juxtaposition of other colours. Thus a scene studied with isolated attention to the details is apt to wear a hardness and harshness which do not reproduce the scene as it appears to the eye.

The three founders of the Brotherhood elected into the fraternity Woolner the sculptor, the painter James Collinson, F. G. Stephens, since well known as an art critic, and W. M. Rossetti, who was to uphold the principles of the Brotherhood in literature, and was appointed Secretary. Madox Brown would not join, saying bluntly that he disapproved of coteries. But, in spite of Rossetti's urgent desire, it appears that he was not actually invited, on the grounds of age, the "grimly grotesque" character of his works, and the fact that he did not render natural objects with sufficient minuteness. Stephens had already some acquaintance with early art; but Woolner and Collinson had none and acquired little. In fact, it may be said that it was the fidelity and simplicity of early art, rather than its archaic character, which attracted the Brotherhood.

The principles of the Brotherhood embraced literature as eagerly as art, a fact which is sometimes lost sight of. Indeed, we find Millais, in the Journal of the P.R.B., hard at work upon a poem.

There ensued a time of boundless aspiration, enthusiastic companionship, and vivid discussion. The members were all comparatively poor men, and their festivities were of the simplest description. "Each man of the company," says Mr. W. M. Rossetti, "even if he did not project great things of his own, revelled in poetry or sunned himself in art." "Rossetti," says Mr. Holman Hunt, "had then perhaps a greater acquaintance with the poetical literature of Europe than any living man. His storehouse of treasures seemed inexhaustible."

Mr. Hunt and Collinson (who was at this time a Roman Catholic) had a strong Christian bias; but the dominant influence of Rossetti held the attention of the Brotherhood closely upon art and literature.

One point is important. It was strongly held in the Brotherhood that purity of mind and heart was a necessary condition for good work, and all that was gross or sensual was strictly tabooed. It is clear that this band of enthusiasts were men of untainted lives, and though they probably had little respect for purely conventional morality, they had a deep-seated desire for nobility of life and aim.

Mr. W. M. Rossetti kept a diary of the work and progress of the Brotherhood, which has been published. But the passages which would probably have cast most light on the proceedings of his brother have disappeared. At some period about 1855, Rossetti inspected the book, and arbitrarily tore out and mutilated a number of pages.

The Brotherhood settled down sturdily to work. Rossetti had chosen as his subject *The Girlhood of Mary Virgin*, a picture on canvas thirty-three by twenty-five inches. Mr. Holman Hunt describes his method of working. "When he had once sat down and was immersed in the effort to express his purpose, and the difficulties had to be wrestled with, his tongue was hushed, he remained fixed, and inattentive to all that went on about him; he rocked himself to and fro, and at times he moaned lowly or hummed for a brief minute."

In 1849 Millais and Hunt had a picture each in the Academy, and Rossetti one in the "Free Exhibition" near Hyde Park Corner. These pictures were well received, the P.R.B. initials which appeared on the pictures being passed over without comment. Rossetti received a brief laudatory notice in the *Athenæum*. *The Girlhood of Mary Virgin* is called "a manifestation of true mental power" with "a dignified and intellectual purpose." The picture was sold to the Dowager Marchioness of Bath, in whose family Miss Charlotte Polidori, Rossetti's aunt, was governess, at his own price.

But in 1850 it was far different. Rossetti's picture *Ecce Ancilla Domini*, now in the Tate Gallery, was exhibited in the National Institution. Rossetti, who had a great deal of trouble over this picture, used to refer to it humorously as "the blessed white eyesore," or "the blessed white daub." At the same time the meaning of the mystic initials P.R.B. was divulged, and the members were wrathfully chastised. The *Athenæum* published a very severe criticism of Rossetti's picture, in which it took occasion to lecture the Brotherhood collectively. They were said to ignore all the great principles of art, and to be "the slavish imitators of artistic inefficiency." Rossetti's picture was called crotchety, puerile, pedantic, affected, absurd. The face of the Virgin was said to be ill-drawn, and that of the Angel insipid. The picture was said to be "a work evidently thrust by the artist into the eye of the spectator more with the presumption of a teacher than in the modesty of a hopeful and true aspiration after excellence." The *Times* wrote in somewhat the same strain, but recognised the picture as the work of a poet. Millais and Mr. Holman Hunt received still harsher treatment. In 1851 the *Times* attacked the work of the Pre-Raphaelite school still more vehemently, speaking of "affected simplicity, senile imitations of a cramped style, false perspective, crude colours, morbid infatuation, and the sacrifice of beauty, truth, and genuine feeling, to mere eccentricity."

This drew from Ruskin two letters to the *Times* (May 13 and 30), in which he bore strong testimony to the "truth, power, and finish" of the pictures,— "both as studies of drapery and of every minor detail," he said, "there has been nothing in art so earnest or so complete as these pictures since the days of Albert Dürer." The immediate cause of the letters was the fact that Coventry Patmore found that Millais was in great distress and agitation at the attacks made upon him, and went straight off to Ruskin begging him to use his influence in the cause of justice.

These letters, "as thunder out of a clear sky," as Mr. Hunt said, turned the current of public feeling. Mr. Hunt, who had been proposing to emigrate to Canada as a farmer, set to work on the *Hireling Shepherd*, and Millais on his *Ophelia*, the face being drawn from Miss Siddal, whom Rossetti afterwards married.

Rossetti about this time designed his great picture *Found*, a picture which stands apart from the bulk of his pictorial work as *Jenny* does from his poetical writing, as a picture of a *genre* order. It is certainly his most characteristic Pre-Raphaelite work, perhaps his greatest achievement, though it was never completed.

But just at this time, when Rossetti, from a practical point of view, should have been throwing himself with full energy into his artistic work, he turned aside to poetry : he wrote or rewrote *Sister Helen, The Bride's Prelude, Dante at Verona, A Last*

Confession, *Jenny*, *The Burden of Nineveh*, and other poems that belong to his finest work. These poems were written easily, but slowly improved upon, with innumerable retouchings.

This desultory neglect of his professional work, so characteristic of Rossetti in his earlier days, and so unlike his later habits, drew from his father strong and sharp remonstrances. Rossetti never took blame easily, though he replied affectionately enough, in a letter which has been preserved; but then and afterwards his affectionate nature grieved over the fact that their relations had ever been strained. But the vexation of Gabriele Rossetti was not unnatural. He was himself incapacitated from work, and the household was mainly depending upon the unremunerative attempts of Mrs. Rossetti and her two daughters to give Italian lessons. Rossetti acquiesced, and wrote in 1852 that he had abandoned poetry.

The interest of the Pre-Raphaelite period is twofold. It is partly that so many of the group rose to high eminence afterwards; but the scene has an intrinsic beauty of its own. It has the eternal charm of generous and enthusiastic youth. Rossetti steps out, like Ion on the temple platform with the virginal freshness of the opening day about him, intent upon his holy service. To read of these days, untainted by passion, unshadowed by the sombre clouds that darken the later life of even the most generous spirits, is like listening to young and careless voices breaking the stillness of the morning air in some enchanted landscape of falling streams and dewy thickets. The practised and patient effort of later days, when faithful hand and brain wrought out into substance those youthful dreams, is perhaps a nobler spectacle; but it is like a draught of fresh spring-water to recall the life of so gifted and hopeful a circle, and to revive the ardent dreams of youth in all their incomparable brightness and strength.

The *Germ* was an enterprise of the Pre-Raphaelite Brotherhood which owed both inception and execution to the stubborn mind of Rossetti. The idea was to publish a sixpenny monthly magazine which was to be φωνᾶντα συνετοῖσιν. It was not to aim at blowing a loud and rebellious blast, at attacking existing institutions and modes of thought, however unenlightened; it was rather to hold up an example of how art should be treated—humbly, faithfully, reverently. It was to be a *Seed*, as one of the latest rejected titles ran, or a *Scroll*, as the last suggestion stood, containing a prophetic message. Eventually the *Germ*—a curiously infelicitous title both in sound and association—was selected. It may be said to be one of the few instances where Rossetti's extraordinary instinct for impressive titles failed to make itself felt. Rossetti's first suggestion was to call it *Thoughts towards Nature*, which was abandoned as being cumbrous as well as affected. Each number was to contain prose, both original and critical, poetry, and an etching. There was a sonnet by Mr. W. M. Rossetti, reprinted on the title-page of each number, which states the principles of the brotherly band so clearly and gracefully that some of it may be quoted—

"When whoso merely hath a little thought
    Will plainly think the thought which is in him—
    Not imaging another's bright or dim,
Not mangling with new words what others taught;

When whoso speaks, from having either sought
　Or only found,—will speak, not just to skim
　A shallow surface with words made and trim,
But in that very speech the matter brought . . ."

The sonnet goes on to deprecate hasty and contemptuous criticism, but bids the spectator ask himself patiently, "Is this *truth*?" The productions of the Brotherhood were thus to be things independently seen or conceived, and independently, not imitatively, expressed, with fidelity and patience.

The first number contained some remarkable writing. There were two poems by Woolner of considerable originality and charm, *My Beautiful Lady* and *Of my Lady in Death*; an interesting essay, *The Subject in Art*, by J. L. Tupper, which though without form, and written in a singularly breathless prose, like an extempore address, is full of suggestive ideas. Coventry Patmore contributed a beautiful little poem; Christina Rossetti a couple of lyrics, afterwards famous. Rossetti himself sent *My Sister's Sleep*, and a very interesting prose romance, *Hand and Soul*, which will be considered later in detail. On the last page was a species of pronouncement as to the principles of the magazine, "to encourage and enforce an entire adherence to the simplicity of Nature."

Not more than two hundred copies of the seven hundred of the first issue were sold. The second number was even less successful. Its most famous contribution is *The Blessed Damozel*, which will be considered elsewhere.

After the comparative failure of this number, it became clear that the finances of the Brotherhood were no longer equal to the strain of publication.

But two more numbers were brought out by the friendly printing firm, the Tuppers, and the title was changed to *Art and Poetry: Being Thoughts towards Nature.*

Among the poetical contributions to the third number appear *From the Cliffs: Noon*, by D. G. Rossetti, afterwards rechristened *Sea Limits*, and a beautiful poem *The Carillon*, written on a tour in Belgium. There is a certain gauntness and stiffness about this, and an almost childish simplicity of phrase; but it has the charm of directness and freshness in a singular degree. It appears in the collected works under the title of *Antwerp and Bruges.* The last number contains six sonnets by D. G. Rossetti on various pictures. Of these the most famous is *A Venetian Pastoral, by Giorgione.* The alterations made in this sonnet at a later date are so interesting and characteristic that one may be quoted. The concluding lines ran originally—

"Let be :
Do not now speak unto her lest she weep,
Nor name this ever. Be it as it was :
Silence of heat and solemn poetry."

In 1869, just before Rossetti issued his *Poems* (1870), he wrote a long letter consulting his brother on various critical points and projected alterations. He had rewritten the concluding lines of the sonnet thus—

"Let be :
Say nothing now unto her lest she weep,
Nor name this ever. Be it as it was,
Life touching lips with immortality."

He adds the following interesting comment on the last line :—

". . . The old line seems to me quite bad. 'Solemn

poetry' belongs to the class of phrase absolutely forbidden, I think, *in* poetry. It is intellectually incestuous, — poetry seeking to beget its emotional offspring on its own identity. Whereas I see nothing too 'ideal' in the present line. It gives only the momentary contact with the immortal which results from sensuous culmination, and is always a half-conscious element of it."

A few words may be said about the etchings which appear in the *Germ*. One was prepared by Rossetti for No. 3, to illustrate *Hand and Soul*, which had appeared in the first number; but Rossetti was so much dissatisfied with the proof that he characteristically tore it up and scratched the plate over. Madox Brown came to the rescue with an etching of Cordelia in *King Lear*.

The *Germ* presents no typographical attractions. It is feebly printed and is adorned with poor thin black-letter headings. Yet this little magazine, a set of which is a rare bibliographical curiosity, has a significance of a very marked kind. It is all fragrant of sincere and enthusiastic youth and artistic purpose. It suggests a whole background of ardent impulsive figures, inspired by a generous emotion, and determined to see things with their own eyes and to say them in their own way. Thus though the little pages are glorified by the distinction which so many of the group afterwards achieved, the *Germ* has a real and intrinsic value of its own.

Rossetti at this period often shifted his quarters. He gave up the studio in Cleveland Street which he had shared with Hunt; and it is odd that in 1849 he should have looked at the house, 16 Cheyne Walk,

Chelsea, in which he was afterwards to live for nearly twenty years. He went to 72 Newman Street, where, a distraint being levied for rent, the effects of Rossetti were seized to make good the landlord's default. He then went to 74 Newman Street, still sleeping at home. In 1851 he took with a friend, Deverell, a first floor at 17 Red Lion Square, and then for a time shared Mr. Madox Brown's studio at 17 Newman Street. But at the end of 1852 he moved into 14 Chatham Place, Blackfriars Bridge, a house now demolished. Here he had a studio, a sitting-room and a bedroom with a fine outlook on the river, and here he remained for nearly ten years.

In 1854 began a close friendship with Ruskin which lasted for several years. On April 14th of that year Rossetti wrote to Madox Brown: "McCracken[1] of course sent my drawing [*Dante Drawing an Angel in Memory of Beatrice*] to Ruskin, who the other day wrote me an incredible letter about it, remaining mine respectfully (!!), and wanting to call. I of course stroked him down in my answer, and yesterday he called. His manner was more agreeable than I had always expected. . . . He seems in a mood to make my fortune."

Ruskin was then nearly ten years older than Rossetti. The two men were of course in a very different position: Rossetti was poor, young, and comparatively unknown; Ruskin was wealthy and eminent in the artistic and literary world. He formed a very high estimate of Rossetti's powers, and behaved to him with extraordinary generosity, making an arrangement whereby up to a certain sum he would

[1] A Belfast shipping-agent, who was a purchaser of Rossetti's pictures.

purchase any of Rossetti's paintings of which he approved.

In 1855 Ruskin wrote: "It seems to me that, amongst all the painters I know, you on the whole have the greatest genius, and you appear to me also to be—as far as I can make out—a very good sort of person. I see that you are unhappy, and that you can't bring out your genius as you should. It seems to me then the proper and *necessary* thing, if I can, to make you more happy, and that I should be more really useful in enabling you to paint properly and keep your room in order than in any other way."

This arrangement put Rossetti in a secure position, and left him free to work as he liked. It is doubtful whether the arrangement was wholly salutary for the young artist. He was acutely sensitive to criticism, and it may be questioned whether this species of "protection" did not tend to stunt his artistic development. Indeed it seems to have confirmed his dislike of public exhibition, for from this time forth he never sent any of his work to any of the ordinary galleries.

Ruskin seems to have constituted himself a kind of amiable mentor to Rossetti, both artistically and practically. He found liberal fault, in a good-humoured, fussy old-maidish way, with his methods of drawing and his use of pigments, and strove to inculcate habits of orderliness and diligence. The letters which he wrote Rossetti have been preserved and are highly entertaining.

Thus he wrote in October 1854:—

"I forgot to say also that I really do covet your drawings as much as I covet Turner's; only it is useless self-indulgence to buy Turner's, and useful self-indulgence to buy yours. Only I won't have them after they have been more than nine times rubbed entirely out—remember that."

Again—"You are a conceited monkey thinking your pictures right when I tell you positively they are wrong. What do *you* know about the matter, I should like to know?"

"Please put a dab of Chinese white into the hole in the cheek and paint it over. People will say that Beatrice has been giving the other bridesmaids a 'predestinate scratched face'; also a white-faced bridesmaid behind is very ugly to look at—like a skull or body in corruption."

Again—"You are a *very* odd creature, that's a fact. I said I would find funds for you to go into Wales to draw something I wanted. I never said I would for you to go to Paris, to disturb yourself and other people, and I won't.

"I am ill-tempered to-day. . . . I don't say you do wrong, because you don't seem to know what *is* wrong, but do just whatever you like as far as possible—as puppies and tomtits do. However, as it is so, I must think for you."

It was hardly possible that with Rossetti's nature this relation should have continued. The wonder is that it lasted so long. At first, no doubt, Rossetti accepted criticism from Ruskin from a consciousness of the high prestige which the latter enjoyed, and also, no doubt, being won by the tender and loving character of the man. But Rossetti had an intense individuality of his own, believed in his own methods, or rather perhaps knew his own limitations; and as he became more secure in his own line, was no doubt less and less inclined to brook paradoxical criticism or fantastic dictation. No doubt he held his own, though his replies have not been preserved; but there was not much in common *au fond* between the two men.

The friendship gradually died away without any definite rupture, and Rossetti went on his way alone. It is interesting to note that Ruskin afterwards said to a friend, that one of the main reasons which made him abjure the society of Rossetti, was that Rossetti dominated him intellectually to such an extent that he could not think his own thoughts when he was with him. After Rossetti's marriage there was but little intercourse, though Ruskin wrote in 1860 :—

"I think Ida" (Mrs. Rossetti) "should be very happy to see how much more beautifully, perfectly, and tenderly, you draw when you are drawing *her* than when you draw anybody else. She cures you of all your worst faults when you only look at her."

Ruskin made some attempts to draw the widening gap together after Mrs. Rossetti's death. Thus in 1862 he wrote :—

"I do trust that henceforward I may be more with you—as I am able now better to feel your great powers of mind, and am myself more in need of the kindness with which they are joined. . . . I've been thinking of asking if I could rent a room in your Chelsea house."

The last suggestion came to nothing. In 1865 Ruskin began to be aware that a gradual severance was taking place. He wrote :—

'[Your letters] conclusively showed me that we could not at present, nor for some time yet, be companions any more, though true friends, I hope, as ever.

... I do not choose any more to talk to you until you can recognise my superiorities as *I* can yours. And this recognition, observe, is not a matter of will or courtesy. You simply do not see certain characters in me. ... A day may come when you will be able. Then—without apology—without restraint—merely as *being* different from what you are now—come back to me, and we will be as we used to be."

After 1868 they never met again, though occasional letters passed between them. So died away this remarkable friendship. Great as Rossetti's tenderness was in the presence of a friend, he was too much preoccupied with his work and his own thoughts to be pre-eminent for loyalty unless there was some natural tie of relationship or close association.

I do not imagine that Rossetti, in spite of his extraordinary power of attaching others to himself, was apt to recur, with wistful affection, to those whom he had known and loved. This defect of sympathy may be held to be frequently characteristic of the strongly developed artistic nature, and Rossetti was one who pre-eminently lived in the present and in the dreams of the day.

To return to our main narrative, an interesting little episode of the year 1854 was that Rossetti, infected by Ruskin's enthusiasm, volunteered to take a class in the Working Men's College, presided over by F. D. Maurice, in Great Ormond Street. Ruskin, in *Præterita*, says generously, "It is to be remembered of Rossetti with loving honour, that he was the only one of our modern painters who taught disciples for love of them."

Rossetti himself wrote to W. B. Scott: "You think I have turned humanitarian perhaps, but you should see my class for the model! None of your *Freehand Drawing-Books* used! The British mind is brought to bear on the British *mug* at once, and with results that would astonish you." His method was characteristic: he put a model—a bird or a boy—before his class, and said "Do it." He did not begin with light and shade, but gave his pupils full colour at once.

In 1857 Rossetti was brought into contact with another interesting group of men, and it is remarkable to observe how he stepped at once into a position of intellectual and emotional dominance among them. He was desired by Ruskin to do some designing work in connection with the Oxford Museum in 1855 which had been placed in the hands of the architect Benjamin Woodward. In 1857 he accompanied Woodward to Oxford, and saw the new debating room of the Union Society. He at once formed the idea of organising some co-operation in an attempt to adorn the bare wall-spaces with frescoes, or, more strictly, tempera pictures. He had in the previous year made the acquaintance of Burne-Jones and William Morris, and these were at once enlisted. Morris had pressed the Arthurian legends upon Rossetti's attention, and Rossetti determined that the Arthurian legend should yield subjects for the frescoes.

The project resulted in a melancholy failure. None of those engaged had had any experience in mural painting; the walls were damp; the brickwork was merely covered with whitewash, and on this surface the frescoes were painted with small brushes, in tempera. The result is that the paintings were speedily obliterated, and now glimmer like ghosts on the walls. Rossetti's own fresco, "Sir Lancelot's Vision of the

Sangrail," was never finished; but it was by common consent considered the finest of the series, belonging, as Burne-Jones said, "to the best time and highest character of his work." The figure of Lancelot was drawn from Burne-Jones himself—a sketch of the design exists. Lancelot lies asleep, while the Grail passes, borne by angels, and Queen Guinevere stands with arms outstretched before an apple-tree.

But the most interesting part of the episode is the light which it throws on the influence which Rossetti established over men like Burne-Jones and Morris. It is recorded of the former that he once introduced a friend to Rossetti, telling him beforehand, "We shall see the greatest man in Europe." Morris was himself an extraordinarily self-willed and independent character. Yet for a time he was completely carried off his feet by Rossetti's influence.

Burne-Jones was the first to succumb to the spell. He was then at Oxford, and destined for the Church, but had begun to make pen and ink designs on his own account, and having conceived a high idea of Rossetti's powers, called upon him and showed him some of his drawings. Burne-Jones's account of their first meeting is so remarkable that it may be quoted here:—

"On the night appointed, about ten o'clock, I went to Lushington's rooms, where was a company of men, some of whom have been friends ever since. I remember Saffi was there, and a brother of Rossetti's. And by-and-bye Rossetti came and I was taken up to him and had my first fearful talk with him. Browning's *Men and Women* had just been published a few days before, and some one speaking disrespectfully of that book was rent in pieces at once for his pains and was dumb for the rest of the evening, so that I saw my hero could be a tyrant, and I thought it sat finely upon him. Also, another unwary man professed an interest in metaphysics; he also was dealt with firmly; so that our host was impelled to ask if Rossetti would have all men painters, and if there should be no other occupation for mankind. Rossetti said stoutly that it was so. But before I left that night, Rossetti bade me come to his studio next day. It was at the top of the last house by Blackfriar's Bridge, at the north-west corner of the bridge, long ago pulled down to make way for the Embankment; and I found him painting at a water-colour of a monk copying a mouse (*Fra Pace*) in an illumination. . . . He received me very courteously, and asked much about Morris, one or two of whose poems he knew already, and I think that was our principal subject of talk, for he seemed much interested about him. He showed me many designs for pictures; they tossed about everywhere in the room: the floor at one end was covered with them and with books. . . . No one seemed to be in attendance upon him. I stayed long and watched him at work, not knowing till many a day afterwards that this was a thing he greatly hated, and when, for shame, I could stay no longer, I went away, having carefully concealed from him the desire I had to be a painter."

The result of this was that Burne-Jones began to paint under Rossetti's guidance; then William Morris was drawn into the net.

The following is Morris's own account of the matter:—

"I have seen Rossetti twice since I saw the last of you; spent almost a whole day with him the last time, last Monday, that was. . . . Rossetti says I ought to paint, he says I shall be able; now as he is a very great man and speaks with authority and not as the scribes, I *must* try. I don't hope much, I must say, yet will try my best—he gave me practical advice on the subject. . . ."

The submissive humility which breathes through

these statements is very unlike the sturdy and burly self-assertion of Morris's later attitude. He devoted himself for a time entirely to painting, and produced some beautifully handled work, in which the minute influence of Rossetti is apparent. Mr. Mackail, in his *Life of William Morris*, says:—

"Rossetti's conquest of a mind so strong and so self-sufficing was, while it lasted, complete in proportion to the strength which was subdued. He became not only a pupil, but a servant. Once, when Burne-Jones complained that the designs he made in Rossetti's manner seemed better than his own original work, Morris answered with some vehemence, 'I have got beyond that: I want to imitate Gabriel as much as I can.' The new gospel was carried down to those of the set who still remained at Oxford, and they were all put to drawing or modelling as if their life depended on it."

There followed a period of close comradeship. The following is Mr. Mackail's account of the habits of the friends:—

"After Burne-Jones went to London at Easter, and began painting under the friendly guidance of Rossetti, Morris used to go up almost every week to spend the Sunday with him at his lodgings in Chelsea. He used to arrive on Saturday in time to see pictures at the Academy or elsewhere, and go to a play with Burne-Jones and Rossetti in the evening. After the play—if Rossetti's imperious impatience of bad acting or bad plays allowed them to sit it out—they would go with him to his rooms on the Embankment overlooking Blackfriar's Bridge, and sit there till three or four in the morning, talking. All Sunday the talking, varied by reading of the *Morte d'Arthur*, went on in the Chelsea lodging, Rossetti often looking in upon the other two in the afternoon. On the Monday morning, Morris took the first train down to Oxford to be at Street's (the architect's) again when the office opened. During these months Rossetti's influence over him grew stronger and stronger. His doctrine that everybody should be a painter, enforced with all the weight of his immense personality and an eloquence and plausibility in talk which all who knew him in those years describe as unparalleled in their experience, carried Morris for a time off his feet."

The reverence with which the two younger men regarded Rossetti is a very remarkable thing. It extended to the smallest details. When they were furnishing rooms, the approval of Rossetti was anxiously awaited. Burne-Jones wrote : " Rossetti came. This was always a terrifying moment to the very last. He laughed, but approved."

It is difficult to estimate the secret of this extraordinary magnetism, which seems almost hypnotic. It was due to the virile independence of Rossetti's character, the determination with which he pursued his own aims, his absolute intellectual indifference, though combined with an acute sensitiveness, to the value of the opinions of others. Then, too, his performances were in the highest degree stimulating. He seemed, as it were, to be in the possession of the innermost and most magical secrets of art. Moreover, he was possessed of a matchless and irresistible eloquence: he did not monopolise the conversation, but his sayings were incisive, fascinating, humorous, and suggestive. At the same time, he displayed a magnificent generosity to the claims of others, and was entirely devoid of any pettiness or envy. No doubt, too, his manner had in those days an irresistible charm : he was tender, genial, and sympathetic. He was apparently unaware of the influence he exerted, and used no arts to gain or maintain it. It is not to be wondered at that the two fell completely under the spell.

Burne-Jones remained a faithful friend and ally

through life, and was one of the few who were welcomed in the inmost circle in the days when from various causes it was narrowing. With William Morris for a long time the association was even closer. Rossetti was a frequent guest in his house at Upton, and was for a time joint-tenant of Kelmscott with him. In Rossetti's later years they seldom met; but though in a sense estranged, there was no definite rupture of relations; a contributing cause being that Morris was a very busy man, and when in London could find little leisure for anything. Another friend of the same date was Mr. Swinburne, who was for a time an inmate of Rossetti's house, and remained a close friend.

From 1870 onwards the diminished intercourse with certain older friends was in a measure compensated for by the devotion of several enthusiastic young men of a later generation, who regarded the friendship of Rossetti as an inestimable privilege. Such, for instance, were Arthur O'Shaughnessy, Philip Bourke Marston, Mr. Fairfax Murray, and Mr. Gosse. The relations of Rossetti to these young men were particularly delightful; he was tenderly paternal in his interest in their work, and spared no pains in helping and advising them. He inspired in them a loyalty and an affection which knew no bounds, and to these late-comers he probably showed less of the capricious side of his character than to his older associates. But after 1877 these friendships, like the earlier ones, felt the overshadowing effects of the darker mood which invaded Rossetti's spirit.

The history of the firm Morris, Marshall, Faulkner and Company, afterwards Morris and Company, in which Rossetti was a partner, demands a few words. It was started in 1861 as a non-limited concern. There were eight original holders, Madox Brown, Rossetti, Webb, Burne-Jones, and Arthur Hughes being the members whose names did not appear. Mr. Hughes withdrew almost at once. Both the inception of the scheme and its original form seem to have been due to Rossetti and Marshall. The members contributed in all £20 each, the rest of the capital being supplied by Morris himself and his mother. The idea was that the members of the firm should be paid for whatever they designed, and this was faithfully carried out. There were no profits for some time, and later on, as the entire direction of the firm fell into the hands of Morris, the tardy profits also passed into his hands. The difficulties of the firm were mainly caused by lack of capital. In 1874 it became clear that the business must be reorganised. The liabilities were unlimited; Morris had embarked all his available capital in it, and devoted the whole of his time to the work. On the other hand, each original member had a legal claim to an equal share of the divisible assets of the firm.

Burne-Jones realised the rights of Morris in the matter, and, with Faulkner and Webb, withdrew; they refused to accept any consideration as partners. Marshall and Rossetti dissented, but accepted the compensation to which they were entitled. Madox Brown throughout strongly opposed the dissolution of the firm. A large sum of money was involved, as the business was beginning to prosper, the stock being valuable, and the goodwill constituting a considerable asset. The details are rather obscure. Mr. William Rossetti says that his brother was on the side of Burne-Jones,

Webb, and Faulkner, and adopted a conciliatory attitude throughout, not desiring any personal compensation. But the members of the opposition section received their due share of the estimated value of the assets and goodwill of the firm. Out of this, a sum of money was certainly assigned to Rossetti, which he laid apart for the eventual advantage of a member of the Morris family, but upon which, before his death, he had trenched to a considerable extent.

It is said that Morris was much hurt at the behaviour of the dissentients. The success of the enterprise was wholly due to him. But it must be in justice admitted that the whole arrangement was a thoroughly unbusinesslike one, and that if the firm had failed, as it was at one time in considerable danger of doing, the others would have been liable to share the pecuniary loss. Madox Brown seems to have always calculated on the profits being eventually an important addition to his earnings; and viewing the matter from a business point of view, it is clear that Morris, as soon as he assumed the direction of the firm, ought to have bought out the other partners. It was hardly equitable that they should have continued to be liable during the earlier years of the firm's existence in the case of possible and indeed probable disaster, and then should have been expected to retire without compensation as soon as the business began to prosper. The result of the winding-up was, certainly, to bring about strained relations between Morris and Rossetti, but as far as feeling went, the rupture was not permanent, though for other reasons the two met no more upon the old footing.

CHAPTER III

LATER LIFE

INTO whatever byways of passion Rossetti may afterwards have strayed, it is certain that his earliest youth was singularly pure. He had no leisure to think of love. It is strange that one whose intellect reached its maturity so early, and in whose conceptions of life Love actual and idealised was to play so unique a part, should have been, on the threshold of manhood, so virginal and even cold in disposition. Probably the intense preoccupation with intellectual and artistic things, combined with the enthusiasm of equal friendship, left but little scope for the approaches of passion. But in 1850 the star of Rossetti's life rose suddenly into the clear heaven.

In that or the previous year W. H. Deverell, a young painter, a genial, brilliant, and romantically handsome young man, doomed to an early death, saw in a bonnet-shop near Leicester Square, working with her needle, a tall dignified girl of extraordinary beauty with a brilliant complexion, pale-blue eyes, and a mass of coppery-golden hair. "She had the look of one," said Madame Belloc, "who read her Bible and said her prayers every night, which she probably did." She speaks also of "an unworldly simplicity and purity of aspect." Deverell through his mother made inquiries as to the possibility of having sittings from the girl, and painted a picture called "The Duke with Viola (Shakespeare's *Twelfth Night*) listening to the Court Minstrels." In this picture Rossetti sat for the head of the Jester, the girl herself appearing as Viola. This strange juxtaposition of two persons whose lives were to be so deeply intermingled is notable. She was then hardly seventeen, her name Elizabeth Eleanor Siddal, daughter of a former Sheffield tradesman. She afterwards sat to Holman Hunt for Sylvia in the picture from *The Two Gentlemen of Verona*, and to Millais for his *Ophelia*.

Rossetti fell at once deeply in love with this quiet self-possessed girl; and an engagement was formed between them in 1851. Head after head in Rossetti's pictures, besides innumerable sketches, give us a very distinct idea of her extraordinary charm. A portrait done by herself in 1853 is not so attractive; the heavy-lidded, somewhat melancholy eyes and the full lips held somewhat primly together have very little of the charm with which Rossetti invested the face. She seems to have had but little education, except what she had acquired for herself; but though thus untaught, and ignorant of many things, she seems to have had a real nobility of spirit, and to have borne herself with dignity and sweetness; but she held, as it were, a certain shield of reserve between herself and the world. She allowed few to suspect what she was —serious, courageous, patient, and loving. She spoke invariably in a dry and humorous vein, neither frivolous nor light, but impenetrable, as though, like St. Francis of Assisi, she said *Secretum meum mihi*—my secret is my own. She was artistically gifted, and had a considerable faculty of poetical invention which is traceable in her drawings; and though the impress of Rossetti's mind and taste is everywhere visible in those pathetic designs, it seems that her own methods to a certain extent affected the character of his work. Mr. Swinburne, defending her from what has been construed into an aspersion upon her in Mr. W. Bell Scott's autobiographical notes, with characteristic generosity says: "It is impossible that even the reptile rancour, the omnivorous malignity, of Iago himself, could have dreamed of trying to cast a slur on the memory of that incomparable lady whose maiden name was Siddal and whose married name was Rossetti." In 1853 traces of a consumptive tendency became apparent, and from that time to the tragic end of her life it was one prolonged struggle with mortal illness.

Rossetti wrote of her in 1854:—

"It seems hard to me when I look at her sometimes, working or too ill to work, and think how many without one tithe of her genius or greatness of spirit have granted them abundant health and opportunity to labour through the little they can do or will do, while perhaps her soul is never to bloom nor her bright hair to fade, but after hardly escaping from degradation and corruption, all she might have been must sink out again unprofitably in that dark house where she was born. How truly she may say, 'No man cared for my soul.'"

In 1854, when Rossetti became acquainted with Ruskin, Miss Siddal was introduced to the latter, and showed him her designs. Ruskin thought her a "noble glorious creature," and made a suggestion which illustrates his chivalrous generosity, that he should settle upon her an annual £150, taking in exchange all the work she did up to that value. Of this arrangement Ruskin wrote: "The chief pleasure I could have about it now would be her simply accepting it as she would have accepted a glass of water when she was thirsty, and never thinking of it any more." In 1855 she consulted Dr. Acland of Oxford, who said that her illness originated in "mental power long pent up, and lately overtaxed." She went abroad for a time and returned no better. The engagement dragged on, Rossetti's finances being still unable to justify marriage, though he was often in her company, even travelling with her in an entirely unconventional brotherly way. It must be confessed that the position was one of great strain. Rossetti, as may easily be supposed, was often acutely jealous, even of his nearest and dearest friends, and avenged any imaginary slight offered to Miss Siddal with extreme displeasure. But in 1860 Rossetti was in easier circumstances, and went with Miss Siddal, then in an extremely delicate condition, to Hastings, where they were married on May 23rd.

They went for a short tour to Paris. It is an inexplicable thing, especially in a man of profoundly superstitious nature, that Rossetti should on his marriage-tour have completed from an early design one of his most impressive drawings, "How they met Themselves," where a lover and his lady, the latter drawn from Miss Siddal, are confronted in a dark woodland by the wraiths of themselves, a presage of death. There is a breathless horror about the picture in its completed form which testifies to the strength of the mood which originated it.

They returned to 14 Chatham Place, some additional rooms being taken in from the adjoining house. Rossetti was now thirty-two, and his habits, rendered inevitable by the characteristic independence of his temperament, were eminently ill-suited for domesticity. He kept what hours he liked, painted when he felt inclined, disliked all questions of economical arrangement, eschewed all ordinary social observances, dashed into restaurants for meals, rather than submit to any domestic routine; he did not attempt to accommodate himself to others, as indeed he had little practice in doing, from the absolute command he had always exercised, down to the smallest details, of the circle in which he lived. At the same time they undoubtedly enjoyed a great if somewhat fluctuating happiness. Rossetti was working very hard owing to an unfortunate event which had taken place in 1860. A Mr. Plint, a nonconformist stockbroker of Leeds, a great admirer of his paintings and one of the most liberal purchasers, died suddenly. He had advanced over £700 to Rossetti on commissions, and the money had flowed out of Rossetti's improvident hands. It was necessary to complete the pictures for the benefit of Mr. Plint's estate, or refund the purchase-money. Rossetti did something of both, and had at the same time to work hard to support his wife and himself. But he managed simultaneously to bring out the *Early Italian Poets*, Ruskin guaranteeing a sum of money to the publishers. Moreover, it was at this time that the Morris firm was constituted, it is thought on Rossetti's suggestion. All this shows under what high pressure he was living. In 1861 Mrs. Rossetti was delivered of a still-born female child, and from that time her health tragically declined. She suffered acutely from neuralgia, and in the later portraits the languor and shadow of death are only too sadly evident. In February 1862 she dined with her husband at a restaurant in Leicester Square. They went back home, and as she appeared to be tired and in pain, he advised her to go to bed; he himself went out to a drawing-class at the Working Men's College. Coming back late he found her unconscious; she had been in the habit, under medical orders, of taking laudanum, and she had miscalculated the dose. Four doctors were summoned, and all was done that could be done. Rossetti, in the course of the ghastly attempts to resuscitate her, went out distractedly to call on Ford Madox Brown at five in the morning: Mrs. Rossetti died an hour or two afterwards. The finding of the coroner's jury was "Accidental Death." Mrs. Rossetti could hardly have hoped that her life, considering her state of health, could have been much prolonged; but it is worse than useless to attempt to speculate as to whether there was any motive in her mind that might have prompted her to self-destruction.

Impar congressus!—it is impossible to resist the feeling that it was an imperfect partnership. There was a certain difference of social standing, to begin with; then, though in mental power and artistic tastes there was a strong similarity between the pair, yet Miss Siddal's lack of formal cultivation put her at a disadvantage in dealing with a mind so impatient of any imperfection of intellectual sympathy as Rossetti's. Again, Miss Siddal's simple religious beliefs were ill-fitted to match with Rossetti's sceptical habit of mind; and lastly, though she was deeply and passionately attached to him, yet the long engagement was a strain on both; and it was moreover a time of sad entanglement for Rossetti, whose sensuous nature gained a firmer hold on him as he grew older. Into the details of Rossetti's wayward impulses it is unnecessary to go; but the jealous hunger of the heart, which is the shadow of devoted love, gave Mrs. Rossetti much cause for unhappiness; and it is enough to say that Rossetti's conscience-stricken condition at his wife's death was based on the knowledge that he had not failed to wound a faithful heart.

Rossetti's demeanour at the inquest and during the sad days before the funeral was extraordinarily courageous and dignified. Just before the coffin was closed he left the room in which some friends were assembled, taking with him a manuscript book of poems, and placed it between the cheek and the hair of his dead wife. He then came back and said what he had done, adding that they had often been written when she was suffering and when he might have been attending to her, and that the solitary text of them should go with her to the grave. It seems that Ford Madox Brown, who was present, thought that this impulsive sacrifice was quixotic, but at such a moment remonstrance was impossible. Rossetti evidently meant it to be a punishment to himself for sacrificing the gentle tendance of love to ambitious dreams, and for even deeper failures of duty, and the volume was buried with his wife in Highgate cemetery that day. The tale of their sad recovery will hereafter be told; but the act has a tragic beauty when one considers what hopes Rossetti thus resigned; and it may be doubted whether in the annals of literature there is any scene which strikes so vehement a note of sorrow and self-reproach—the abased penitence of a strong, contrite, and passionate soul.

After the death of his wife Rossetti felt entirely unable to live any longer at Chatham Place, and eventually took a lease of a house in Chelsea, No. 16 Cheyne Walk, called Tudor House, which is inseparably connected with his life and fame and tragic decline.

It was a large house in what was then a very picturesque and secluded region. There was no embankment then, but all the long-shore bustle of boats and barges. It was an extensive, old-fashioned, comfortable house—too big for a single tenant. There lay a great garden behind it, nearly an acre in extent, with limes and other trees, the thick foliage of which darkened the back windows. Rossetti had a roomy studio at the back, and a bedroom with a small breakfast-room attached. There was a dining-room, and a fine drawing-room on the first floor occupying the whole front of the house; above were a number of bedrooms. Besides Rossetti there were at first three sub-tenants, Mr. Swinburne, Mr. George Meredith, and Mr. William Rossetti. The idea was to lead a kind of collegiate life: Mr. Swinburne and Mr. Meredith had their own sitting-rooms where they received their visitors, and it was understood that all in residence should dine together in the evenings. Mr. Meredith's tenancy did not continue very long; and indeed it required rather peculiar qualities to submit to the rule of a president such as Rossetti was. He was masterful, independent, full of strong prejudices strongly expressed. Though his enthusiasm and genius were great, yet his view both of art and literature was narrowly circumscribed. Moreover, for an experiment of the kind to prove successful, a certain submissiveness with regard to habits, tastes, and hours, or at all events a considerable indifference to settled ways of life, must have been essential. Rossetti himself kept what hours pleased him; he rose late, he took his meals when it suited him, he worked most of the day and went out when he chose, he sat up to unearthly hours of the night. It is true that he was affectionate, generous, and lovable; but he was not considerate in small things, and it is on that quality more than on any other that the harmony of domestic life depends.

It has often been supposed that Rossetti after his wife's death fell into habits of morbid seclusion. This is an entire mistake. He suffered acutely, and from this time forward he was no longer a stranger to moods of great depression. But his vitality was then at its strongest; he worked hard at his painting, he read, he saw much of his particular friends. Moreover, he may be said to have invented the modern taste for old furniture, china, and *bric-à-brac* of every kind. He became an industrious collector, rummaging old curiosity shops and furniture shops in every direction, more for the love of the pursuit than for pleasure in what he collected; he filled the great house with pictures, objects of art, china, and ancient furniture. He bought curious animals, which he kept in the garden: he possessed at one time or another a wombat, a woodchuck, an armadillo, a racoon, a kangaroo, a deer, a chameleon, a salamander, and even a zebu, which last proved to be dangerous. The wombat used to sleep on the epergne in the middle of the dinner-table, entirely indifferent to the talk, the movement, and the lights. On one occasion it took advantage of a particularly enthusiastic and absorbed discussion to descend from its place and gnaw the contents of a box of expensive cigars.

Rossetti's professional income grew very rapidly; in 1865 he made over £2000, in 1876 his income was nearly twice that amount, and he said that he regarded this as about his average. But though he had a strong business capacity, and made excellent bargains for his pictures, he was lavish of money, fond of gratifying every whim, and extremely generous; so that he accumulated very little. He had a taste for wealth, but none for economy. There is a story of his being paid for a picture in notes, and keeping the roll in an unlocked drawer, taking out any sum he wanted. His servants caught the spirit of their master, and the housekeeping was of the most reckless description. He dabbled during these years in spiritualism, and was evidently haunted by a strong desire to prove if possible the continuance of individuality after death.

Occasionally he travelled to Belgium or France, but never left Great Britain after 1864. Perhaps it may be said that the earlier years of his life in Cheyne Walk were his happiest period; he was able to live as he liked; he found his fame and his wealth grow, without the need of modifying or sacrificing any of his idiosyncrasies. He saw those of his friends whom he desired to see, and he found himself full of artistic impulse, which he was able to embody as he desired.

But the shadow began to fall. In 1867 insomnia began to afflict him, and his eyesight showed signs of failing. He was by temperament highly impatient of physical suffering, and was, moreover, so entirely wrapped up in his work, that anything which threatened the suspension of activity was an intolerable calamity. He had practically no recreations; and though in many ways physically indolent, yet he was incapable of deliberate rest, and had no quiet, tranquil occupations in which he could take refuge.

In 1868 he paid his first visit to Penkill Castle, Ayrshire, the home of Miss Alice Boyd, a gifted amateur artist whom he had known for some years. He returned in better health and spirits, though he said that his eyes still troubled him, and that he saw all objects that were not quite close to him with a veil interposed, which he described as being like curling smoke or effervescing champagne. He took to wearing strong glasses, which he never removed. In 1869 he revisited Penkill, and it now became clear that there was some definite nervous mischief at work. He often discussed the ethics of suicide, and was under the impression that he was visited by manifestations which proved that the spirit of his wife was near him. William Bell Scott, who was at Penkill at the time, gives a curious story of a walk which he took with Rossetti to a certain dark pool in a rocky glen near Penkill, when he believed that the prompting to self-destruction visited Rossetti's mind with a sudden insistence. Moreover, Rossetti found a chaffinch in the road to Girvan, which allowed itself to be picked up, handled, and carried home, and which he seems to have in some way connected with the spirit of his wife. But his intellect was extraordinarily vigorous. He wrote several poems, among them *The Stream's Secret*, one of his most musical and mystical lyrics, much of which he composed in a cave by the side of the brown, rushing Penwhapple, near Penkill. He recollected and recovered by memory many of his early poems, the only copy of which was in his wife's grave. His friends had several times urged him to recover the MS.; Rossetti resisted, but at last, fretted by his inability to remember the poems, he yielded. The matter was arranged with the Home Secretary, Mr. Bruce, afterwards Lord Aberdare. One night, seven and a half years after the funeral, a fire was lit by the side of the grave, and the coffin was raised and opened. The body is described as having been almost unchanged. Rossetti, alone and oppressed with self-reproachful thoughts, sat in a friend's house while the terrible task was done. The stained and mouldered manuscript was carefully dried and treated, and at last returned to his possession. He had the poems copied out, and destroyed the volume. But it is impossible to resist a certain feeling of horror at the episode. Rossetti was not a man to have yielded tamely to the suggestions of friends in this or any other matter; such grace as belonged to the original act was forfeited by the recovery of the book; and there is a certain taint about the literary ambition which could thus violate the secrecy of the grave, however morbid the original sacrifice may have been.

The poems were eventually published in 1870, and it is characteristic of Rossetti that he was careful to provide that the book should be reviewed, in prominent periodicals, by personal friends of his own, who should not err by want of sympathy with the author's treatment. Even William Morris went so far as to write, in the *Academy*, what was perhaps the only review of his life.

The book was received with a chorus of approval. Mr. Swinburne wrote a generous panegyric in the *Fortnightly Review*, and at first there was hardly a dissentient voice. Rossetti stepped at once into the front rank of contemporary poets. Seldom has there been a more easy and complete triumph. No doubt a certain mysterious prestige already surrounded the author. Very little was known about him; his pictures were never exhibited, but commanded the admiration of the best connoisseurs. He was known, too, to be at the centre of a group of interesting and commanding personalities, and some reflection of the extraordinary homage which even then was paid him had reached the curious ears of the world. From this period may be said to date the inquisitive interest in the personality of Rossetti, stimulated by the deliberate seclusion in which he lived; and from this period, too, date the curiously exaggerated legends that were circulated about him, of which it is enough here to say that the shadows were far darker than were in the least degree justified by the reality. Rossetti cannot be described as a man who submitted to current views of morality. He loved swiftly and almost unscrupulously; but he was in no sense a profligate; his faults were the faults of passion, not restrained by the ordinary social code.

But the strangest irony of all is that the man who most unaffectedly desired seclusion, and the *fallentis semita vitæ*, who abhorred publicity, and compliments, and distinguished consideration, who desired only to live his own life and dream out his own dreams, should have been subjected to so close and inquisitive a curiosity that it has proved necessary, in order to preserve his memory unstained, to present a closer and more minute picture of his life and habits than has ever perhaps been given to the world of a great personality. It was not that he courted curiosity, as some have done, by denying himself to the general gaze. He had no designs on the admiration or compassion of the world; as long as he could live as he desired, write and paint as he chose, and have the company of those whom he loved, he asked no more. This, indeed, in a sense he achieved; but he could not achieve the lonely self-ordained life which was his deliberate choice.

It is here necessary to say a few words on one of the dark shadows of Rossetti's life—his chloral habit, which began about 1870. Rossetti's unhappy misuse of chloral is generally and radically misrepresented. He is spoken of as the victim of a vicious indulgence which he had not the strength to give up. Of course it cannot be defended; his happiness was wrecked by it, for chloral was no doubt the main cause of the sad delusions that overclouded his later years, and it, moreover, undoubtedly shortened his life. But it must be remembered that his use of it was not to indulge a dangerous pleasure, or for the sensations which it gave him; he took it primarily as a medicine for insomnia, in the unhappy belief that it was innocuous in its results and mechanical in its action. He no doubt at first, and evidently for a long time, thought of himself as a man who must choose between sleeplessness and a potent drug, and that as his livelihood and energies depended upon his getting some measure of sleep, there was no choice in the matter. Given the circumstances, combined with the elements of his character, self-will, impatience of suffering, and entire independence of opinion, there are all the materials for an inevitable catastrophe. It is easy to say he ought to have submitted himself to some strict medical *régime*, but that was exactly what Rossetti would not do, and it is not impossible that insomnia might have precipitated a still worse calamity. There is no doubt that he gradually became aware that he was becoming enslaved to the drug. What he said on the subject to Mr. Hall Caine shows that he knew, a year or two before the end, what havoc it was working on his life and constitution; but by this time he had gone too far to draw back, except by submitting himself to a restraint which he was the last person in the world to accept. Nothing can make it less of a tragedy than it was. It is simply horrible to see one so robust, active, and enthusiastic going slowly down the dark descent with clouded brain and saddened brow; but it is the case of a man confronted in his own thought with a disastrous cessation of the energies upon which his life was built; finding to his intense satisfaction a simple and effectual relief, and then becoming aware that that very specific is taking a fatal hold on him. But there was no conscious sense of degradation connected with it. He wrote and spoke freely to his friends and relations of his attempt to reduce the drug, as a man who finds the treatment of an ailment becoming in itself dangerous. As he wrote to Ford Madox Brown in 1877: "The fact is, that any man in my case must either do as I do, or cease from necessary occupation, which cannot be pursued in the day when the night is stripped of its rest."

I imagine that it was on the medical aspect of the case that his mind mainly dwelt. The delusions of spirit, the weakness of will, the fear of contact with the world were not by himself attributed to chloral;

his insane terror of the conspiracy which he believed existed to decry and to defame him was to him a real and objective thing. If he had found his intellectual powers weakened, and his artistic skill directly diminished by the drug, I believe he would have been far more ready to acquiesce in measures to break off the use of it; but I do not imagine that he himself, until near the end, thought the chloral responsible for his failing constitution; and it seems that when his medical adviser determined that at all hazards the habit must be broken, he did not refuse his consent.

It is therefore a complicated situation; and it is not swiftly and sternly to be dismissed as a case of pernicious and deliberate indulgence in a base form of pleasure. It is not primarily a question of morals, but a case of reckless imprudence in adopting, apart from medical advice, a specific which had such fatal consequences.

In 1871 Rossetti became joint-tenant with William Morris of Kelmscott Manor-House, in Oxfordshire, near Lechlade, and close to the Thames. He introduced a picture of the house in the background of *Water Willow*. It is a large, ancient, pearly-grey building of rubble-stone, "buttered over" with plaster, the stones showing through; many-gabled, mullioned, stone-slated, extraordinarily unspoilt, with farm buildings all about it. It had a beautiful garden with fine yew hedges, and stood near an old-world hamlet. The landscape has all the charm of a secluded river-valley. William Morris loved the place passionately; but Rossetti, though alive to the dreamy charm of the scene, was not at heart a lover of the homely beauty of the earth. To him the smallest touch of human beauty had more significance than the noblest natural prospect.

Rossetti was at Kelmscott during the summer and autumn of 1871, again in the winter of 1872-3, and for the greater part of the following eighteen months. He had written to Madox Brown from Kelmscott in 1869 :—"One might settle down into complete and most satisfactory habits of work here. There are two splendid riverside walks to be taken alternately every day, without a soul to be seen on the road to disturb the cud of composition, and at home everything lends itself to poetic composition." There is a big upper room at Kelmscott hung with tapestry representing the story of Samson. Here Rossetti worked, though he was much fretted by the insistence of the design. In the summer of 1874 he finally left it, and Morris continued to occupy it alone. The association of these two great names with the house will always give it a special sanctity.

But he was not an easy inmate. A friend visiting him at Kelmscott in 1874 found him dining at 10 P.M., and not going to bed till four or five in the morning. His health was bad, and he was much beset by morbid delusions and suspicion of harmless persons. Moreover, he thought that the isolated position of the place was ill-adapted for making professional arrangements for disposing of his pictures. The immediate cause of his departure was a strange quarrel with some anglers, who, he morbidly thought, had insulted him on purpose.

It was a relief to Morris when Rossetti abandoned Kelmscott. From the first almost he had been "unromantically discontented" with it: "he has all sorts of ways so unsympathetic with the sweet simple old place that I feel his presence there as a kind of slur on it."

In some ways the family life there had been happy enough. Rossetti was devoted to the Morrises and their children, who found him a delightful playmate. But where he loved, he loved jealously and passionately, and the situation was an uneasy one. It may be added that the great friendship of Rossetti's life dates from this period. Mr. Theodore Watts, now Watts-Dunton, a man of letters, a poet, a novelist, and a critic, made Rossetti's acquaintance over a legal matter, and to the end of his life was his most devoted friend. It would be impossible to exaggerate the value of his friendship for Rossetti. Mr. Watts-Dunton understood him, sympathised with him, and with self-denying and unobtrusive delicacy shielded him, so far as any one can be shielded, from the rough contact of the world. It was for a long time hoped that Mr. Watts-Dunton would give the memoir of his great friend to the world, but there is such a thing as knowing a man too well to be his biographer. It is, however, an open secret that a vivid sketch of Rossetti's personality has been given to the world in Mr. Watts-Dunton's well-known romance *Aylwin*, where the artist Darcy is drawn from Rossetti.

But it is now necessary to turn to an incident of the year 1871 which was fruitful in disaster for Rossetti. In the *Contemporary Review* for October 1871 appeared an article, afterwards expanded into a pamphlet, entitled "The Fleshly School of Poetry—Mr. D. G. Rossetti." The article was signed Thomas Maitland, and was written by the poet recently deceased, Robert Buchanan. The morality of this device has been impugned, and it is true that a personal attack of this character should have been anonymous rather than pseudonymous. Into all the stages of the painful affair it is not necessary to go. At first Rossetti did not appear to be particularly disturbed by the attack. He wrote a very temperate reply under the title of *The Stealthy School of Criticism*, portions of which appeared in the *Athenæum* over his signature. But Buchanan was not content, and early in 1872 he issued his article expanded into a pamphlet, in a far more extended and denunciatory form.

The *Fleshly School of Poetry* was a strong, coarse onslaught, grossly unjust and intolerably vehement, but gaining in venom and power to wound from the fact that it was an attack made in the shape of a defence of public morality. No doubt the defence was prompted by sincere motives; but both the furtive method employed, and the deliberate injustice by which Rossetti was selected as a typical example of the decadent school, were inexcusable. The attack was pointed by quotation; but by carefully selected quotations it would be as easy or easier to prove both Shakespeare and Milton to be vile and shameless poets, undermining the foundations of morality. The whole tone and spirit of Rossetti's poems are misrepresented. It is true that there breaks out in places a certain voluptuousness of phrase and image, but the fault is rather one of taste, in speaking without disguise of things more wisely left to men's memories and hearts, but not in themselves either unnatural or debasing; of recounting things, which, as Horace says, are *sacro digna silentio*. Indeed, it is too strong to say *taste*; it should rather be English taste; and it must be kept in mind that Rossetti was by instinct an Italian, and that though he was deeply versed in English literature, and a master of English speech, one can never think of him as a purely English poet; he never learned to look at things from an English point of view. The Englishman's idea of love-making is of a secretive order, and just as, in conversation, a sturdy silence, for instance, about religious things is not inconsistent with a deep religious devotion, so the experiences of love are to an Englishman more suited for memory and recollection and seclusion, not *sub divum rapienda*, though the ardours of passion may be deeply felt and regarded as a very high and holy mystery of sweetness. Possibly the instinct may be wrong, and Englishmen would not lose in self-respect by a greater candour about the deeper experiences of life. But it is a national instinct for all that, and not to be lightly defied. In any case, the harm was done. There were innumerable people who agreed with the spirit of Buchanan's attack, who never endeavoured to verify for themselves the truth of his accusation, nor heeded his recantation. For Buchanan, writing to Mr. Hall Caine after Rossetti's death, said: "I was unjust, as I have said; most unjust when I impugned the purity and misconceived the passion of writings too hurriedly read and reviewed *currente calamo*; . . . I make full admission of Rossetti's claims to the purest kind of literary renown." Yet the result is now that a certain cloud hangs, in popular opinion, over Rossetti's writings; and the immediate effect upon himself was to cause him deep pain, to unsettle his sensitive mind, and to contribute in no small measure to the disaster of his later life.

The charges, if they were true, were sufficient to create a deep suspicion of Rossetti among virtuous and respectable people. What passed in Rossetti's thoughts cannot be known; but his brother discovered, on visiting him in June 1872, that his mind was unhinged. He became the victim of a delusion, from which he never entirely recovered, that there was a widespread and carefully organised conspiracy on foot against him to hound him out of society; the smallest things fed this unnatural idea. He received a presentation copy of *Fifine at the Fair* from Robert Browning, fastened upon some lines at the end as a veiled attack upon himself, and at once expunged Browning from the number of his friends. He believed that Lewis Carroll's *jeu d'esprit*, *The Hunting of the Snark*, was a satire upon himself. Medical advice was summoned, and Rossetti consented to go to the house of a friend, Dr. Hake. Here he swallowed the contents of a phial of laudanum that he took with him, and his life was with difficulty preserved. He was, on recovery from the poison, discovered to be afflicted with partial paralysis of the leg. He was finally removed to Scotland, his friends rallying round him in a way which testifies to the wonderful loyalty which he inspired. He spent some time in Perthshire, at Urrard and Stobhall, two houses belonging to Mr. William Graham, M.P., the purchaser of many of his pictures. He was then moved to Trowan, near Crieff, where he made a rapid recovery, and resumed his painting. He continued, however, to take chloral. To meet his immediate necessities his great collection of china was sold, producing a large sum of money; and towards the end of September 1872 he was well enough to go down to Kelmscott, where he recovered to a great degree his spirits and energy. He wrote to his brother, September 25, 1872: "The pleasant peaceful hours at Euston Square yesterday were the first happy ones I have passed for months; and here all is happiness again, and I feel completely myself." But his delusions never wholly left him.

After leaving Kelmscott, as has already been related, he returned to Cheyne Walk, and resumed his usual habits of life and work. In 1875 he took a house for a time at Bognor, called Aldwick Lodge, and then went for a while to Broadlands, the hospitable house of Lord Mount-Temple.

But his painful hallucinations continued to beset him. Whether he was tricked by his own fancy, or merely misinterpreted ordinary sounds is not clear, but he was often under the impression that cabmen and other strangers insulted him; airy voices taunted him with epithets of intolerable ignominy; even a thrush which sang insistently in his garden was believed by him to have been trained to ejaculate terms of obloquy to annoy him. Yet his intellectual vigour was absolutely undimmed; his conversation, when he could keep off the dangerous subject, was still vigorous, fascinating, and stimulating. He painted as deftly and suggestively as ever, and wrote with the same entire command of forcible and beautiful English.

In 1877, after a severe and painful attack of illness, from a complaint to which he was subject, he went down to a little place called Hunter's Forestall, in Herne Bay, and here he gave way to deep depression, imagining that he would no longer be able to design or paint. But his wonderful vitality again came to his assistance, and he returned to town with renewed energies. Yet all this time he was gradually increasing the doses of chloral, and took a certain ghastly pride in the amount he could consume. The shadow darkened and deepened. In 1879, a friendship with Mr. Hall Caine brought for a time a little light into his life. Mr. Hall Caine's *Recollections* of Rossetti is one of the most interesting and fascinating pieces of literary biography of modern times. Rossetti showed himself to him on terms of unguarded and brotherly intimacy, and Mr. Caine's book depicts the closing scenes of a memorable life in a way that, with all its wealth of detail, is never anything but dignified and stately. In July 1881, Mr. Caine became a regular inmate of the house, a position involving great strain, very loyally borne.

In the early part of that year, Rossetti was preparing a new issue of his 1870 *Poems*, adding the work that had since accumulated. He ultimately divided the material into two volumes, *Ballads and Sonnets*, and *Poems*, both of which were issued at the end of 1881. In *Ballads and Sonnets* appeared *Rose Mary*, *The White Ship*, and *The King's Tragedy*, the completed *House of Life*, and certain other new lyrics and sonnets. Into the revised *Poems* some fresh work was introduced, notably the unfinished early poem, *The Bride's Prelude*. The reception of these volumes was uniformly respectful, and even enthusiastic; but no evidence of cordial admiration could give Rossetti, in his failing state, any increase of cheerfulness or satisfaction.

I may here quote two or three of Mr. Hall Caine's reminiscences :—

"I should have described Rossetti, at this time, as a man who looked quite ten years older than his actual age, which was fifty-two, of full middle height and inclining to corpulence, with a round face that ought, one thought, to be ruddy but was pale, large grey eyes with a steady introspecting look, surmounted by broad protrusive brows and a clearly-pencilled ridge over the nose, which was well cut and had large breathing nostrils. The mouth and chin were hidden beneath a heavy moustache and abundant beard, which grew up to the ears, and had been of a mixed black-brown and auburn, and were now streaked with grey. The forehead was large, round, without protuberances, and very gently receding to where thin black curls, that had once been redundant, began to tumble down to the ears. The entire configuration of the head and face seemed to me singularly noble, and from the eyes upwards, full of beauty. He wore a pair of spectacles, and, in reading, a second pair over the first: but these took little from the sense of power conveyed by those steady eyes, and that 'bar of Michael Angelo.' His dress was not conspicuous, being however rather negligent than otherwise, and noticeable, if at all, only for a straight sack-coat buttoned at the throat, descending at least to the knees, and having large pockets cut into it perpendicularly at the sides. This garment was, I afterwards found, one of the articles of various kinds made to the author's own design. When he spoke, even in exchanging the preliminary courtesies of an opening conversation, I thought his voice the richest I had ever known any one to possess. It was a full deep baritone, capable of easy modulation, and with under-tones of infinite softness and sweetness, yet, as I afterwards found, with almost illimitable compass, and with every gradation of tone at command, for the recitation or reading of poetry. . . .

"Dropping down on the sofa with his head laid low and his feet thrown up in a favourite attitude on the back, which must, I imagine, have been at least as easy as it was elegant, he began the conversation by bantering me upon what he called my 'robustious' appearance compared with what he had been led to expect from gloomy reports of uncertain health. After a series of playful touches (all done in the easiest conceivable way, and conveying any impression on earth save the right one, that a first meeting with any man, however young and harmless, was little less than a tragic event to Rossetti) he glanced one by one at certain of the topics that had arisen in the course of our correspondence. I perceived that he was a ready, fluent, and graceful talker, with a remarkable incisiveness of speech, and a trick of dignifying ordinary topics in words which, without rising above conversation, were so exactly, though freely enunciated as would have admitted of their being reported exactly as they fell from his lips."

The following is a memorable scene :—

"Before going into my room he suggested that I should go and look at his. It was entered from another and a smaller room which he said that he used as a breakfast room. The outer room was made fairly bright and cheerful by a glittering chandelier (the property once, he told me, of David Garrick), and from the rustle of trees against the window-pane one perceived that it overlooked the garden; but the inner room was dark with heavy hangings around the walls as well as the bed, and thick velvet curtains before the windows, so that the candles in our hands seemed unable to light it, and our voices sounded thick and muffled. An enormous black oak chimney-piece of curious design, having an ivory crucifix on the largest of its ledges, covered a part of one side and reached to the ceiling. Cabinets, and the usual furniture of a bedroom, occupied places about the floor: and in the middle of it, and before a little couch, stood a small table on which was a wire lantern containing a candle which Rossetti lit from the open one in his hand—another candle meantime lying by its side. I remarked that he probably burned a light all night. He said that was so. 'My curse,' he added, 'is insomnia. Two or three hours hence I shall get up and lie on the couch, and, to pass away a weary hour, read this book'— a volume of Boswell's *Johnson* which I noticed he took out of the bookcase as we left the studio. It did not escape me that on the table stood two small bottles sealed and labelled, together with a little measuring-glass. Without looking further at it, but with a terrible suspicion growing over me, I asked if that were his medicine.

"'They say there is a skeleton in every cupboard,' he said in a low voice, 'and that's mine; it is chloral.'

"When I reached the room that I was to occupy during the night, I found it, like Rossetti's bedroom, heavy with hangings, and black with antique picture panels, with a ceiling (unlike that of the other rooms in the house), out of all reach or sight, and so dark from various causes that the candle seemed only to glimmer in it—indeed to add to the darkness by making it felt."

In the following passage Mr. Caine describes his first sight of Rossetti:—

"Very soon Rossetti came to me through the doorway in front, which proved to be the entrance to his studio. Holding forth both hands and crying 'Hulloa,' he gave me that cheery, hearty greeting which I came to recognise as his alone, perhaps, in warmth and unfailing geniality among all the men of our circle. It was Italian in its spontaneity, and yet it was English in its manly reserve, and I remember with much tenderness of feeling that never to the last (not even when sickness saddened him, or after an absence of a few days or even hours) did it fail him when meeting with those friends to whom to the last he was really attached."

The following account of his conversation has great interest:—

"A certain incisiveness of speech which distinguished his conversation, I confess myself scarcely able to convey more than a suggestion of; as Mr. Watts has said in the *Athenæum*, his talk showed an incisiveness so perfect that it had often the pleasurable surprise of wit. Rossetti had both wit and humour, but these, during the time that I knew him, were only occasionally present in his conversation, while the incisiveness was always conspicuous. A certain quiet play of sportive fancy, developing at intervals into banter, was sometimes observable in his talk with the younger and more familiar of his acquaintances, but for the most part his conversation was serious, and, during the time I knew him, often sad. I speedily observed that he was not of the number of those who lead or sustain conversation. He required to be constantly interrogated, but as a negative talker, if I may so describe him, he was by much the best I had heard. Catching one's drift before one had revealed it, and anticipating one's objections, he would go on from point to point, almost removing the necessity for more than occasional words. Nevertheless, as I say, he was not, in the conversations I have heard, a leading conversationalist; his talk was never more than talk, and in saying that it was uniformly sustained yet never declamatory, I think I convey an idea both of its merits and limitations."

It is impossible not to be struck by the fact that every one who has any personal recollection of Rossetti lays particular emphasis on the marvellous beauty of his voice and enunciation. Its wonderful resonance, its profound *timbre*, seem to have exercised a species of physical influence over his auditors. As Mr. Caine says, of his reading of *The White Ship*:—

"It seemed to me that I never heard anything at all matchable with Rossetti's elocution: his rich deep voice lent an added music to the music of the verse: it rose and fell in the passages descriptive of the wreck with something of the surge and sibilation of the sea itself; in the tenderer passages it was soft as a woman's, and in the pathetic stanzas with which the ballad closes it was profoundly moving. Effective as the reading sounded in that studio, I remember at the moment to have doubted if it would prove quite so effective from a public platform. Perhaps there seemed to be so much insistence on the rhythm, and so prolonged a tension of the rhyme sounds, as would run the risk of a charge of monotony if falling on ears less concerned with points of metrical beauty than with fundamental substance. Personally, however, I found the reading in the very highest degree enjoyable and inspiring."

In September 1881, Rossetti, being much out of health and in great depression of mind. was induced to accompany Mr. Hall Caine to a house in the Vale of St. John, near Keswick, and regained some slight degree of physical activity. He even ascended a mountain in the neighbourhood; but his dejection returned with redoubled force. His companion wrote: "At that time of the year the night closed in as early as seven or eight o'clock, and then in that little house among the solitary hills his disconsolate spirit would sometimes sink beyond solace into irreclaimable depths of depression." They came back to Cheyne Walk in October, and Rossetti said with deep feeling, as he was helped across the threshold, now feebler than ever, "Thank God! home at last, and never shall I leave it again." The depression continued, and he became very anxious, though a pronounced agnostic, for confession and absolution. It was suggested to him that this was contrary to his pronounced views, to which he replied, "I don't care about that. I can make nothing of Christianity, but I only want a confessor to give me absolution for my sins!" adding, "I believe in a future life. Have I not had evidence of that often enough? Have I not heard and seen those that died long years ago? What I want now is absolution for my sins, that's all!" But he did not carry out his intention.

He still worked on, without any marked diminution of technical skill. But the end was close at hand. He had a species of paralytic stroke in December 1881, and it was decided that the chloral must be summarily cut off. This was done under careful medical precautions. After a short period of intense suffering he regained calmness of mind, and entire freedom from delusions. He recovered sufficiently to be able to resume work, and even to call several times at his mother's house in Torrington Square; but a fatal illness that had long threatened him supervened. A friend lent him a bungalow at Birchington, and he went down there to try and regain strength. But he never really revived. At first he walked a little, and worked fitfully at his painting; he finished a grotesque ballad, *Jan Van Hunks*, begun more than thirty years before, which he used to read aloud in the evenings with great amusement. He read novels and wrote a few letters. But the spring of life was broken, and his brother wrote in a diary that on April 1 he was "in a very prostrate condition physically, barely capable of tottering a few steps, half blind, and suffering a good deal of pain." On April 8, Saturday, he said to his brother, "I believe I shall die to-night," adding, "Yesterday I wished to die, but to-day I must confess that I do not." About 9.30 on the evening of Easter Sunday he was seized with convulsions and died in a few minutes, in the presence of his mother, brother, and sister, Mr. Watts-Dunton, and Mr. Caine. He was within a few weeks of completing his fifty-fourth year.

He was buried quietly on April 14, 1882, at Birchington, where a cross has been erected over his grave.

Rossetti was in appearance more Italian than English, though rather conveying an indefinable impression of foreign origin than displaying markedly foreign characteristics. He was of medium stature, not more than five feet eight inches; he was thin in youth, and in maturity decidedly stout. His complexion was clear and dark, his hair dark, silky, and abundant. There was a great depth and breadth of brow, he had small ears, and white, delicate, womanly hands. As a young man he wore only a moustache; but after he was thirty he grew thin whiskers, and a rather straggling beard of a dark brown tint.

But what made his face remarkable was the expression. The full, blue-grey, wide-open eyes, in cavernous bistred sockets, the large, distended nostril, the loose under-lip wore a look that indicated fire, determination, and energy. He walked rapidly and resolutely, though of a lounging and indolent habit indoors. There are several well-known portraits of him; a youthful one (by himself), with abundant hair, has a certain look of Keats. When he grew his beard he resembled Hoccleve's miniature of Chaucer. He sat to F. M. Brown in 1851 for the head of Chaucer in the large picture of *Chaucer reading to the Court of Edward III. the Legend of Custance*, and some have said that this is one of the best portraits of him. A portrait by Mr. G. F. Watts conveys the impression of incisiveness rather than strength. But the best known of all, which are acknowledged to be the most faithful likenesses, are two or more photographs taken by Downey in 1862. In one of these,—a full-face, —the heavy mouth, the sunken eyes, the deep indentation above the nose, give a sort of bull-like look of strength; while the wide nostril and the set seriousness of the brow lend to the expression a dictatorial and peremptory look, a kind of *sæva indignatio* which is highly impressive.

There is a picture, the original by Mr. Dunn, for some years Rossetti's assistant, of extraordinary interest and fidelity, which is reproduced in Mr. Watts-Dunton's *Aylwin* (4th edition, 1899), representing

Rossetti lounging in a chair in the green dining-room of the Cheyne Walk house, reading from a manuscript to Mr. Watts-Dunton, who sits on a sofa at his side.

Rossetti has given several interesting particulars about his method of composition. He wrote easily in youth, but it was a long, deliberate, and exhausting process in his later days. He speaks in one of the Kelmscott letters of finding the lonely walks there favourable to composition, and at Penkill he wrote a good deal seated in the open air. He told a friend that his poetry took a great deal out of him. "In that respect," he said, "I am the reverse of Swinburne. For his method of production inspiration is indeed the word. With me the case is different. I lie on the couch, the racked and tortured medium, never permitted an instant's surcease of agony until the thing on hand is finished." And again, he said of the composition of the *King's Tragedy*, "It was as though my life ebbed out with it." And of *Rose Mary* he said "that it had occupied three weeks in the writing, and that the physical prostration ensuing had been more than he would care to go through again." In 1881 he sent a sonnet to his sister, for his mother to read, adding, "With me, sonnets mean insomnia." But this strain seems to have been absent in earlier years. His early letters from abroad are full of poetry, some narrative, some lyrical; and there is no hint that they cost him any particular effort, but rather came freely from an active mind, overflowing with zest for all beauty, whether of form or colour, word or phrase.

It is interesting, however, to observe that his most

mature work was thus carefully and fastidiously shaped. He left some prose sketches of intended poems, but they are the barest outline, as in the draft called *The Orchard Pit*, published in the *Collected Works*; the detail and phrasing were left to the moment. He altered and retouched a good deal, but mostly in proof; he did not feel (and he was like Tennyson in this respect) that he really knew what was the worth and colour of a poem till he saw it in print. He submitted his poems a good deal to those of his intimates whose opinion he valued, but desired frank criticism more than suggestion.

Rossetti was a great but not a wide reader; he read entirely for pleasure and not for information, as a relaxation and not as a pursuit. His tastes were purely literary; he cared nothing for history, politics, or science. His knowledge of English poetry was very great in certain limited directions, and his memory for it was minute and accurate. He could quote large masses by heart. Yet he cared nothing for certain departments of literature, such as the Elizabethan dramatists. His tastes were eclectic, as may be imagined, and he had a keen eye for everything that bore the impress of strong individuality, for everything that was original, bizarre, unusual, grotesque, and peculiar. He was within certain limits a penetrating and incisive critic, but with strong preferences and prejudices, and it was difficult to forecast what his judgment would be. There is an amusing story of William Morris sending him some proofs of *Sigurd the Volsung*, which Rossetti expressed himself unable to read. Morris pressed him for his reasons, and Rossetti said with languid indifference that he really could not take any interest in a man whose parent was a snake. This petulant and perverse dictum from the author of *Lilith* provoked Morris to vehement wrath, and he exploded in a gross personal retort. Though singularly independent in judgment, it is clear that, at all events in the later years of his life, Rossetti's taste was, unconsciously, considerably affected by the critical preferences of Mr. Watts-Dunton. I have heard it said by one who knew them both well that it was often enough for Mr. Watts-Dunton to express a strong opinion for Rossetti to adopt it as his own, even though he might have combated it for the moment.

His admiration of Chatterton may be held to have been somewhat extravagant. Again, he always maintained of Oliver Madox Brown, the gifted son of Ford Madox Brown, who died at the age of twenty, that his name would be a familiar one in English literature. But allowing for these lesser deviations, the fact remains that Rossetti had a very masculine judgment and a profound critical insight. He was not, of course, in the technical sense of the word, a critic. It was rather a supreme power of divining what was forceful and beautiful that he possessed—

> "What is best
> He firmly lights upon, as birds on sprays."

But he had little sense of comparison or systematic synthesis. His favourite writers seem to have been Shakespeare, Keats, and Coleridge, whom he classed as the three great English imaginations. For Keats indeed he had an overpowering admiration, writing of him as "the one true heir of Shakespeare." He had studied the early English ballads in his youth very carefully, and remarked once that he had said to himself on realising their variety and majesty, "There lies your line." He had a great love of Milton's sonnets, but unduly underrated Wordsworth. Browning had at one time a great fascination for him. He spoke of Blake, Donne, and Tennyson Turner in terms of high praise. He was a constant student of Dante and the early Italian poets, and in Italian prose he was an admirer of Boccaccio. He was much attracted by the writings of E. A. Poe, both verse and prose. In English prose he was a great reader of Boswell's *Johnson* and of Dickens; but his favourite fiction was Dumas, of whom he possessed some hundred volumes. He had at one time carefully studied Swedenborg. He was fond of out-of-the-way literary biographies, such as Hogg's *Shelley* and Cottle's *Coleridge*. His library was mostly for use, and was collected on no plan. He possessed only about a thousand volumes: among these were a certain number of rare books and bibliographical curiosities. He was a slow and careful reader, and much given to writing marginal annotations in his volumes.

CHAPTER IV

POEMS—CHARACTERISTICS

IN the poetry of the nineteenth century it may be roughly said that two strains have chiefly predominated. The strongest impulse has perhaps been the impulse to annex philosophical speculation to poetry, to find a poetical solution for the problem lying behind nature and life, or to turn to account emotions of a philosophical kind. The other notable element has been the poetry of human relations and affections in their most direct forms. With neither of these had Rossetti any close affinity. Here again it is necessary to remind ourselves that he was not in any sense an Englishman, though he used the English language for his medium of expression. He belonged in reality to the mediæval school of Italian poetry; he was entirely unaffected by national problems, by the expansion of scientific and philosophical ideas. In an age which dealt largely with abstractions, he had no affinity with abstract thought. To him the emotions and the experience of life lay entirely in the intricate and complex development of human passion, the mysterious relations of human spirits; but even here he did not approach the thought from its abstract side. For him human passion was inextricably connected with its outward manifestations, in the emotions stirred by the apprehension of beauty alike definite and indefinite, the gracious mysteries of which human form and features, gesture, movement, and glance seem a sacramental expression. This was not in Rossetti's case a purely material sentiment; all these outward lovelinesses seemed to him to hide a secret, to be the very voice of some remote spirit speaking instantly to the soul.

As he wrote himself in the *Athenæum*, December 16, 1871, of a certain sonnet in the *House of Life*, which had been chosen as a *point d'appui* of the most deliberate attack ever made upon him:—"Any reader may bring any artistic charge he pleases against the above sonnet; but one charge it would be impossible to maintain against the writer of the series in which it occurs, and that is, the wish on his part to assert that the body is greater than the soul. For here all the passionate and just delights of the body are declared—somewhat figuratively, it is true, but unmistakably—*to be as naught if not ennobled by the concurrence of the soul at all times.*" Or again, as he wrote in memorable words, embodying the innermost secret of his creed, of the type of beauty that he made his own—

"Whose speech Truth knows not from her thought,
Nor Love her body from her soul."

That was Rossetti's message. The underlying truth is greater and more beautiful than any human expression of it; but just as, under earthly limitations, a philosophical conception cannot exist apart from the words in which it is expressed, so to Rossetti the material expression of beauty was the only key to its mystery, and, for the present at least, indissolubly connected with it.

The soul then, in pursuit of this secret, must be alive to any hint that comes to it from the beauty of outward form. That was, then, the task of his life—*the embodiment of mystical passion.*[1]

It was this strict limitation of Rossetti's emotion and thought that gave him his peculiar power. Nearly all his poems are the expression of some poignant passion; his tragedies are the tragedies of blighted or broken love, and the blind recklessness that follows upon it. His view of nature is as a background, either of similarity or contrast, to the emotions which are being enacted in the foreground. Woods and hills are accessories: even in such poems as *The Stream's Secret*, where the stream passes, as it were, through the forefront of the dream, it is charged with the message and tidings of far-off love. The voice of the beloved is heard within the ripple, and the murmur of the water seems to be trying to convey to the listening brain some hint of passion.

In his earlier days he seems to have held that painting had a possible future, while "English poetry was fast reaching the termination of its long and splendid career, and that Keats represented its final achievement." This theory he used to maintain with rhetorical force and vehement conviction. Speaking to Burne-Jones in the summer of 1857, he said, over and over again, "If any man has any poetry in him he should paint, for it has all been said and written and they have scarcely begun to paint it."

At first poetry was to Rossetti but a recreation to be taken in the intervals of painting; but it gradually

[1] See *The Truth about Rossetti*, by Theodore Watts, *Nineteenth Century Review*, March 1883.

absorbed his mind, and he began to see that there was abundant room for it in the world. Thus in 1871 we find him writing from Kelmscott to Ford Madox Brown: "I wish one could live by writing poetry. I think I'd see painting d——d if I could."

His theory of writing, as originally formed, was to find the most direct and unconventional expression possible for what had to be said. At the same time he had a strong feeling of the dignity of language requisite for poetry. As Mr. Hall Caine says: "Rossetti himself constantly urged that in prose the first necessity was that it should be direct, and he knew no reproach of poetry more damning than to say it was written in proseman's diction." He abhorred all intricacy of style, and held that absolute lucidity of expression was the first necessity. His constant emendations were directed, not always successfully, to the same end, to strengthen and clarify. In the earliest poems the result is a certain gauntness and stiffness of expression which is not without its charm, but is alien to his latest manner. Sometimes this precision of delineation carried him too far, as, for instance, in the stanza of which Coventry Patmore, speaking of the "fierce light of imagination" which Rossetti threw upon external things, wrote that it "seems scratched with an adamantine pen upon a slab of agate:—

> 'But the sea stands spread
> As one wall with the flat skies,
> Where the lean black craft, like flies,
> Seem well-nigh stagnated,
> Soon to drop off dead.'"

This stanza of *Even So*, obviously conceived under the

influence of Browning, finds its first sketch—by no means a rough one—in Rossetti's description in a letter of the "dense fogs of heat" at Hastings.

"Emphasis and condensation," it is said, "were the characteristics of his muse." "I hate long poems," he often declared, and of Sydney Dobell he once impatiently enunciated, "What a pity it is that he insists on being generally so long-winded." Yet, as we shall have occasion to point out, he was not always true to this principle. He might emphasise and condense a particular stanza; but there are poems like *The Bride's Prelude*, and *Dante at Verona*, where the mood is too much drawn out.

Rossetti's poems, then, were based upon some clearly seen pictorial impression of a dramatic moment; occasionally, for a longer poem, he made a prose sketch of the line he was intending to follow. But the actual creation of the visible form was absorbing, and demanded all the powers of his mind. He would have differed *toto cœlo* from the breezy maxims of William Morris, who said of writing poetry, "That talk of inspiration is sheer nonsense, I may tell you that flat; there is no such thing: it is a mere matter of craftsmanship. . . . If a chap can't compose an epic poem while he's weaving tapestry, he had better shut up, he'll never do any good at all."

Walter Pater, in his essay in Ward's *English Poets*, makes what I believe to be a paradoxical criticism on Rossetti's poetry. He says that "his meaning was . . . in a certain sense learned and casuistical." I confess that I fail to catch hold of the clue that would lead me to this conclusion. In the ordinary sense of the word, casuistical implies a certain bewilderment in the presence of the moral issues of action or thought; and a casuist in art would be a man who found his idea of beauty complicated by a difficulty in defining where the essence of beauty lay, whether Nature provided an ultimate test, whether moral excellence had any voice in the matter, whether human associations could exercise a certain selection, and whether there were any absolute canons of beauty at all.

Into these metaphysical regions I do not think that Rossetti entered. Strong as his sense of beauty was, it was not in the least a catholic sense. If a thing or a thought struck him as beautiful, beautiful it was to be; and I imagine that he was impervious both to suggestion and argument. His only preoccupation was to find due expression for what visited him in the form of an inspiration.

The result of his experience in his art can be very plainly traced. He had two perfectly distinct manners. In his earlier period, when beauty of the world opened before him, he had both in his poetry and his pictures a sweet and exquisite *naïveté* of phrase and conception, that "first fine careless rapture" which gives the world, one is tempted to think, the best and most uplifting art, the art that springs from a pure natural joy, and uses words and colours with something of the bright insouciance of a child, unhampered by criticism and tradition alike.

Then, as the years went on, and this natural freshness became dimmed by sad experience, by mental and physical suffering, the growing strength of the craftsman comes to his aid; the earlier, simpler, more direct manner is discarded, and he begins to spin gorgeous word-textures, strange tapestries of language and colour, which in his writings resulted in the construction of what is literature rather than poetry.

Rossetti was saved by his intensity of view and his firmness of conception from ever falling a victim to expression pure and simple. But setting a sonnet out of the *House of Life*, with its reverberating roll of sound, against such a delicate poem as *The Portrait*, or a picture of some ideal female head like the *Astarte Syriaca*, with all its dark jewellery of colour, against an early water-colour like *Fazio's Mistress*, one feels that technical advance is not pure gain. Full to the brim as the later work is of all that art can do, it is like placing some gorgeous confection, to which a hundred strange exotic products have contributed their scents and savours, side by side with a branch plucked from some orchard tree, laden with virginal fruit, with the dew of the morning still globed upon it.

The deep melancholy traceable in so many of the poems is inseparable from Rossetti's later view of life. The mystery of death, of separation, of the decay and vanishing of charm, of pain and sorrow, cutting in, so to speak, across the message of beauty, could not be shut out from his thoughts. To him such things were not pathetic; they did not hint at possibilities of restoration and future fulfilment. They seemed rather like a relentless tempest, sweeping from some evil and boding quarter, rending and wrecking the perfection, the sweetness, the loveliness of life. He did not probe deeper, and try to discover some formula which could harmonise and glorify the horror. He merely said, "Though the heart ache to contemplate it, it is there."

Rossetti's use of words is an interesting study. In his early poems he had a strong fancy for archaic words which pleased him by a certain richness of form, such as "galiot," "cote-hardie," "chevesayle and mantelet," "stound," "grout," and so forth. With this went an ancient simplicity and directness of phrase, and a tendency to use monosyllabic and Anglo-Saxon words. But in the *House of Life* the precise opposite is the case. Here he chose to employ a great variety of double words, a tendency perhaps traceable to his love for Keats, such as "we late-tottering world-worn hence," "dawn's first hill-fire," "winter-bitten, angel-greeted door," "wing-winnowed," "sky-breath and field-silence," and so forth. Together with these are a certain number of exotic words not always even correctly derived, such as culminant—gracile—lovelihead—unfeatured—garmented—queendom. Moreover in the sonnets he had a fancy for using great resonant classical words, with a certain roll of sound, such as "Night's inveteracy," "multiform circumfluence manifold," "auroral wind," "firmamental blue," "life's confederate pleas," "June's encomiast." We find such lines as "the unfettered irreversible goal," "Sleepless with cold commemorative eyes." Note such textures as—

"Oh! what is this that knows the road I came,
  The flame turned cloud, the cloud returned to flame,
    The lifted shifted steeps and all the way?—
  That draws round me at last this wind-warm space,
  And in regenerate rapture turns my face
    Upon the devious coverts of dismay?"

Or

"Ah! who shall dare to search through what sad maze
  Thenceforth their incommunicable ways
  Follow the desultory feet of death?"

It will be observed in these last quotations there is a certain slight shifting of the usual meanings of words like *commemorative*, *regenerate*, and *incommunicable*, some slight nuance added to them which is not found in ordinary speech. This preciosity has a charm of its own, and upon this handling of language, this delicate straining of the use of words, depends much of the pleasure derivable from the work of masters of elaborate style.

Rossetti composed his later sonnets carefully, working the metal with endless elaboration, frequent retouching, so as to cover every space with beauty. It remains that he is a master in both kinds of writing, though, perhaps, he is at his best when he is neither archaic nor elaborate.

There is one very marked characteristic of Rossetti's lyrical writing which deserves special attention. It is what, to use a technical musical phrase, may be called his "*attack*." The lyric, or the sonnet, breaks upon the ear in a strong, arresting phrase, which at once puts the mind in tune for what follows. Such is the fine, abrupt opening of *The Staff and Scrip*—

> "'Who rules these lands?' the Pilgrim said.
>   'Stranger, Queen Blanchelys.'
> 'And who has thus harried them?' he said.
>   'It was Duke Luke did this:
>   God's ban be his!'
>
> The Pilgrim said: 'Where is your house?
>   I'll rest there, with your will.'
> 'You've but to climb these blackened boughs
>   And you'll see it over the hill,
>   For it burns still.'"

The sonnets contain even more notable instances, which it would be easy to multiply. Such lines as—

"Girt in dark growths, yet glimmering with one star"

from *Sleepless Dreams*; or—

"Look in my face; my name is Might-have-been;
I am also called No-more, Too-late, Farewell";

from *A Superscription*, are of the same type.

The tendency of the sonnet-writer as a rule is to reserve such effects for the climax; but it is a truer economy to arouse the spirit at the outset as by a pealing trumpet-note, though such magnificence is only possible to writers of exuberant richness. It is notable, on looking through Rossetti's sonnets, how many of them have this massive opening. It is a real note of his most deliberate style. It is as when one waits in the stillness for the sounding of some far-off chime. At last the murmur, sweet as honey, comes softly brimming over, like water from an overflowing vessel slowly filled. Then the music topples delicately down, till the great hour-bell, in its wise, grave voice, proclaims the flight of time, and the hour is told.

Another characteristic of Rossetti's writing, standing side by side with the gorgeousness both of word and phrase which he attained by such curious felicity, is the effect of dignity achieved by the severest simplicity, by the profuse employment of monosyllabic words.

This is well exemplified by the close of an early sonnet, not wholly successful, *On the Field of Waterloo*, which is redeemed from a certain ungainliness by the splendid close—

> "Am I to weep? Good sirs, the earth is old:
> Of the whole earth there is no single spot
> But hath among its dust the dust of man."

Again, in the admirable termination he put to the ancient stanza, *How should I your true-love know?—An Old Song ended*, comes a quatrain which reads even more like the work of his sister, in its almost child-like simplicity of phrase—

> "'For a token is there nought,
>   Say, that he should bring?'
> 'He will bear a ring I gave
>   And another ring.'"

But it is, perhaps, in the sonnets that the most notable effects of this kind are to be observed. In the following extracts it may be noticed that for the closing line the very simplest and shortest words are employed. Thus, from *Retro me, Sathana!*—

> "Thou still, upon the broad vine-sheltered path,
> Mayst wait the turning of the phials of wrath
> For certain years, for certain months and days."

And again, from *The Hill Summit*, an early sonnet—

> "And see the gold air and the silver fade
> And the last bird fly into the last light."

And still more exquisitely in the closing two lines of *The One Hope*, a sonnet which he ranked with his very best work, where the contrast with the more ornate lines that precede makes the simple dignity more forcible—

> " Ah! when the wan soul in that golden air
>   Between the scriptured petals softly blown
>   Peers breathless for the gift of grace unknown,—
> Ah! let none other alien spell soe'er
> But only the one Hope's one name be there,—
>   Not less nor more, but even that word alone."

These extracts are sufficient to show that even in these latter days, when simple words have been worn threadbare by use, there is still room for perfect simplicity, and that the outfit is not too slender for the large enterprise.

Rossetti's rather robust humour was as a rule carefully excluded from his poems. It is interesting to study from this point of view the different versions of *The Burden of Nineveh*, originally cast in a semi-humorous mould, and to see how the satirical passages fell out one by one.

Another characteristic in which Rossetti exercised a severe restraint is that of pure fantasy. That he had it strongly developed there is no doubt. Such a whimsical sonnet as *A Match with the Moon*, where he "dogged the flying moon with similes," is a grotesque, like a Bewick, and shows a vivid imagination almost, as it were, in a fever-fit—

> " Like a wisp she doubled on my sight
>   In ponds, and caught in tree-tops like a kite
>   And in a globe of film all liquorish
>   Swam full-faced like a silly silver fish ;—
>   Last like a bubble shot the welkin's height . . ."

But it is clear that this was a species of juggling with art which Rossetti felt to be undignified, for such experiments are excluded, as a rule, from his published work.

Rossetti had a mood, to which he gave way but sparingly, of making words into a kind of vague music. As a rule, the conception dominates him; but there are poems which are like a sweet modulation, where the effect is produced not by the adaptation of the words to the central thought, but by a species of murmuring melody, in which the thoughts seem blurred upon the edge of a gentle slumber. Such pre-eminently is *Love's Nocturn*—

> "There the dreams are multitudes:
> Some that will not wait for sleep,
> Deep within the August woods;
> Some that hum while rest may steep
> Weary labour laid a-heap;
> Interludes,
> Some, of grievous moods that weep.
>
> Poets' fancies all are there:
> There the elf-girls flood with wings
> Valleys full of plaintive air;
> There breathe perfumes; there in rings
> Whirl the foam-bewildered springs;
> Siren there
> Winds her dizzy hair and sings."

Such a line as "Valleys full of plaintive air" attains perhaps the highest beauty which such slumberous art can reach.

A word must be said of Rossetti's use of the supernatural. It played a large part in his ballads; but here too he shows his art in the vigilant restraint which he imposed upon himself. There is nothing melodramatic about his use of it; but the wind blows cold out of the inner shrine of fear. In the early poem *The Portrait* is a passage, chosen, by some incomprehensible error, by Buchanan, to illustrate the thesis that Rossetti's writing was "formally slovenly and laboriously limp," but which stands in the very first rank of the poetry that brings a sense of dim mystery and remote horror to the mind—

> "In painting her I shrined her face
> 'Mid mystic trees, where light falls in
> Hardly at all ; a covert place
> Where you might think to find a din
> Of doubtful talk, and a live flame
> Wandering, and many a shape whose name
> Not itself knoweth, and old dew,
> And your own footsteps meeting you,
> And all things going as they came." [1]

Again, could a certain kind of haunted nightmare and shapeless terror be more powerfully expressed than in this passage from *Love's Nocturn*?—

> "Reft of her, my dreams are all
> Clammy trance that fears the sky :
> Changing footpaths shift and fall ;
> From polluted coverts nigh,
> Miserable phantoms sigh ;
> Quakes the pall,
> And the funeral goes by."

Again, in *Rose Mary*, a poem full from end to end of the subtlest supernatural imagery, the description of

[1] It is interesting to study in the original MSS., as I have been enabled to do by the kindness of Mr. William Rossetti and Mr. Fairfax Murray, the various stages of the careful process by which this particular poem was elaborated. It will suffice here to say that the most characteristic lines of the above stanza are to be found in the earliest draft.

the great Beryl stands out pre-eminent—

> "With shuddering light 'twas stirred and strewn
> Like the cloud-nest of the wading moon :
> Freaked it was as the bubble's ball,
> Rainbow-hued through a misty pall
> Like the middle light of the waterfall."

Another characteristic of Rossetti's writing is the way in which one is suddenly brought face to face, in a few simple words, with an intensity of tragic feeling that leaves the mind breathless with the stress of passion. Such is the moment in *Sister Helen* where the last agonised prayer of the old father, Keith of Keith, for his son's life, falls in vain on the desperate ears—

> "'Oh he prays you, as his heart would rive,
> Sister Helen,
> To save his dear son's soul alive.'
> 'Fire cannot slay it, it shall thrive,
> Little brother !'"

Or the moment when Rose Mary, searching with her eye the imaged landscape for the ambush which she knows lurks somewhere—

> "'Hush, sweet, hush ! be calm and behold.'
> 'I see two floodgates broken and old :
> The grasses wave o'er the ruined weir,
> But the bridge still leads to the breakwater ;
> And—mother, mother, O mother dear !'"

Or again in *The Staff and Scrip*, when the dead warrior is brought back to the queen who had been hoping against hope that he would return in triumph—

> "'Oh what do ye bring out of the fight,
> Thus hid beneath these boughs ?'
> 'Thy conquering guest returns to-night,
> And yet shall not carouse,
> Queen, in thy house.'

'Uncover ye his face,' she said.
'O changed in little space!'
She cried, 'O pale that was so red!
O God, O God of grace!
Cover his face.'"

In the matter of rhyme Rossetti was easily contented. As a rule his rhymes conform to ordinary rules, but there are cases where the weakness of rhyme is difficult to justify. Not to travel far for instances, one finds such rhymes as "of" and "enough" not unfrequently, and—which I think is the lowest level he ever reached—in *Eden Bower* occurs the following—

"'All save one I give to thy freewill,—
The Tree of the Knowledge of Good and Evil,'"

which cannot be defended on any grounds.

The one kind of rhyme which is extremely characteristic of Rossetti is a strong syllable associated in rhyme with a weak one—

"And gay squires stilled the merry stir,
When he passed up the dais-chamber."

(It may be noted, in passing, that he pronounced *dais* as a monosyllable.) And again in *Rose Mary*—

"Nay, the flags are stirred in the breeze,
And the water's bright through the dart-rushes."

These rhymes were used partly deliberately to give a pleasing contrast; but partly, I think, Rossetti's ear gave weak endings a certain emphasis which a purebred Englishman would hardly affix to them. This tendency was skilfully parodied by Buchanan in

The Fleshly School of Poetry—

> " When winds do roar and rains do pour,
> Hard is the life of the sailor :
> He scarcely, as he reels, can tell
> The side-lights from the binnacle :
> He looketh on the wild water."

We are told, it will be remembered, that in Rossetti's reading there was an "insistence on the rhythm," and "a prolonged tension of the rhyme-sounds," which was very noticeable. And such lines as

> " And when the night-vigil was done,"

and

> " Say nothing now unto her, lest she weep,"

which last recalls the tones of Mr. Chadband, are sufficient, I think, to prove, either that he was not fully aware how destitute of emphasis the final syllables of English words tend to be, or that he disapproved of slurring them over, and deliberately adopted a more distinct pronunciation.

In the early poems, written when the Pre-Raphaelite influence was very strong, there is a deliberate *naiveté* of style, a prominence of homely detail, which he afterwards entirely discarded. Such touches as occur, for instance, in *My Sister's Sleep*, show a close power of observation of small accessory effects. Take, for instance—

> " Her little work-table was spread
> With work to finish. For the glare
> Made by her candle, she had care
> To work some distance from the bed."

And again—
> 'Our mother rose from where she sat:
> Her needles, as she laid them down,
> Met lightly, and her silken gown
> Settled: no other noise than that."

But occasionally this early simplicity rises into a stateliness which has a special charm of its own, very different from the gorgeous dignity of his later work. The close of *The Portrait*, written about 1848, is a fine example of the earlier manner—

> "Here with her face doth memory sit
> Meanwhile, and wait the day's decline,
> Till other eyes shall look from it,
> Eyes of the spirit's Palestine,
> Even than the old gaze tenderer:
> While hopes and aims long lost with her
> Stand round her image side by side,
> Like tombs of pilgrims that have died
> About the Holy Sepulchre."

The *Ave*, too, of the same date, has something of the same artlessness—

> "To whose white bed had come the dream
> That He was thine and thou wast His
> Who feeds among the field-lilies."

There is no English poet of the nineteenth century who has so little of the instinctive love of Nature as Rossetti. He was essentially an indoors poet. To begin with, his life, with interludes of practically a few months, except for the time he lived at Kelmscott, was spent in London, and then mostly in his own house. He rose late and worked during daylight. Thus he had but a small store of experiences to draw upon when compared with other English poets of his age. He disliked bodily activity, and even when he did walk, it is recorded that he often seemed to take no particular notice of the world about him. His pleasure in the Kelmscott landscape seems largely to have been built upon the fact that it contained so few disturbing elements.

This tendency, however, gives his poetry a certain strength; he is never tempted to expatiate upon the landscape, but it is always subordinated to the central thought with an artistic restraint which is apt to be violated even by Tennyson himself. Landscape is, in fact, strictly an accessory in Rossetti; and, one is tempted to think, always pictorially conceived.

At the same time, he had the faculty of close and delicate observation when he chose to employ it; and if his eyes had been more trained in recording and storing impressions of Nature, it is clear that he would have excelled in natural description. Scattered up and down his writings are touches of skilful pictorial art, such as—

> "Where the long cloud, the long wood's counterpart
> Sheds doubled darkness up the labouring hill."

Or, what is one of the most carefully studied effects, a great flight of starlings, seen at Kelmscott—

> "Sun-steeped in fire, the homeward pinions sway
>   Above the dovecote-tops;
> And clouds of starlings, ere they rest with day,
> Sink, clamorous like mill-waters, at wild play
>   By turns in every copse.
>
> Each tree heart-deep the wrangling rout receives,—
>   Save for the whirr within,
> You could not tell the starlings from the leaves;
> Then one great puff of wings, and the swarm heaves
>   Away with all its din."

He has a great power of bringing a scene rapidly before the eye by one delicate stroke—as in *Sister Helen*—

> "'Outside it's merry in the wind's wake,
> Sister Helen;
> In the shaken trees the chill stars shake.'
> 'Hush, heard you a horse-tread as you spake,
> Little brother?'"

Again—

> "'Here high up in the balcony,
> Sister Helen,
> The moon flies face to face with me.'"

And again, from the *Last Confession*—

> "And from the fountains of the public place
> Unto the pigeon-haunted pinnacles,
> Bright wings and water winnowed the bright air."

The above all show with what a sure instinct he laid his finger on the one salient feature, and wasted no words about it. Only the best word-artists can afford to show such an austerity of reserve.

The traces of the influence of other poets upon Rossetti are small. His early admiration for Browning is, however, clearly enough indicated in *A Last Confession*. The opening is exactly in the manner of Browning, and many cadences throughout the poem are built up in Browning's semi-conversational style—

> "Our Lombard country-girls along the coast
> Wear daggers in their garters: for they know
> That they might hate another girl to death
> Or meet a German lover. Such a knife
> I bought her, with a hilt of horn and pearl."

There is a trace, I believe, of Coleridge's influence in the *Blessed Damozel*, as will be pointed out.

The Tennysonian influence is hardly perceptible; but in the early poem *The Portrait*, to which allusion has been made, occurs a stanza which might well stand as the work of Tennyson—

> "But when that hour my soul won strength
>   For words whose silence wastes and kills,
> Dull raindrops smote us, and at length
>   Thundered the heat within the hills.
> That eve I spoke those words again
> Beside the pelted window-pane;
>   And there she hearkened what I said,
>   With under-glances that surveyed
> The empty pastures blind with rain."

And that a real and fundamental similarity existed between the poets is exemplified by *The Lady of Shalott*, a poem both in conception and handling strongly resembling Rossetti's work.

Of course the ballads are bound to show traces of the influence of the ballad literature which Rossetti studied so eagerly. But the only ballad which is purely archaic in handling is *Stratton Water*; while of the Euphuistic Jacobean style there is but one trace that I can detect—a couplet in the *Ave* which might have come straight from Crashaw—

> "The cherubim, succinct, conjoint,
>   Float inward to a golden point,"

though it is, of course, an effect studied from early Tuscan painting. These slight traces of Rossetti's style being to any extent, even superficially, affected by literary influence are just enough to show how entirely original his manner was.

Keats, it must be added, was the chosen poet of

the Pre-Raphaelites: they read him, quoted him, and designed pictures from his poems. Perhaps Rossetti's preferences here as elsewhere were dominant; but Keats's whole treatment of a subject was, so to speak, almost typically Pre-Raphaelite. There was the strong conception of the situation, the powerful motive of passion, the chivalrous view of woman, and all set in a framework of exquisite detail, luxuriously lavish, and precisely delineated. Such poems as *The Eve of St. Agnes*—

> " And still she slept an azure-lidded sleep,
> In blanched linen, smooth, and lavender'd,
> While he from forth the closet brought a heap
> Of candied apple, quince, and plum, and gourd;
> With jellies soother than the creamy curd,
> And lucent syrops, tinct with cinnamon;
> Manna and dates, in argosy transferr'd
> From Fez; and spiced dainties, every one,
> From silken Samarcand to cedar'd Lebanon";

and the unfinished *Eve of St. Mark*—

> " The city streets were clean and fair
> From wholesome drench of April rains;
> And, on the western window panes,
> The chilly sunset faintly told
> Of unmatured green, vallies cold,
> Of the green, thorny bloomless hedge,
> Of rivers new with spring-tide sedge,
> Of primroses by shelter'd rills,
> And daisies on the aguish hills.
>
> . . . . .
>
> Her shadow, in uneasy guise,
> Hover'd about, a giant size,
> On ceiling-beam and old oak chair,
> The parrot's cage, and panel square;

> And the warm angled winter-screen,
> On which were many monsters seen,
> Call'd doves of Siam, Lima mice,
> And legless birds of Paradise,
> Macaw, and tender Av'davat,
> And silken-furr'd Angora cat."

are typical instances of subjects treated as the Pre Raphaelites treated them.

CHAPTER V

POEMS—*HOUSE OF LIFE*

THERE are nine poems of Rossetti's that may be called ballads,—though he himself only called three of them ballads, and included the other six among the Poems.

These are *Rose Mary*, in three parts, *The White Ship*, *The King's Tragedy*; and to these we may add *Sister Helen*, *The Bride's Prelude* (unfinished), *The Staff and Scrip*, *Troy Town*, *Eden Bower*, and *Stratton Water*. That is to say, all of these poems include a narrative, though *Sister Helen* is in reality a drama, the whole story being told by two speakers.

Of course it must be admitted that, in the strictest sense of the word, none of these poems are in reality ballads. A ballad is a narrative poem dealing with some contemporary episode, and its characteristics are simplicity and directness. It owes its force to association, sincerity, and a primal impulse of dramatic emotion. A modern ballad must be either an attempt to imitate from a literary point of view existing ballads—*Stratton Water* is an instance of this—or else the using of an archaic and traditional form enriched with later art and colour.

Of Rossetti's ballads *Sister Helen* is the noblest, as *Rose Mary* is the richest. *Sister Helen* is probably the highest achievement of his art. It was written in 1851, and first published in the *Düsseldorf Magazine*, then edited and published in Germany[1] by Mary Howitt. It was issued in book-form with further alterations at Oxford in 1857; and this is the rarest, perhaps, of all Rossetti's publications. Some small additions were made in 1870, but the 1881 edition was considerably amplified. Interesting as the question of the additions is, it is not proposed to discuss them here.[2] It will suffice to say that the interpolations are all improvements, though few of them quite rank with the best of the original stanzas.

The *motif* of the poem is that of a woman in a lonely hill-castle melting the waxen image of her false lover, and the arrival of his brother, his father, and his wedded wife to pray for mercy; but she persists in her task to the dreadful end. The poem is a conversation between Helen herself and her little brother, who is set in the window to watch what may befall, while the slow agony is in progress.

Each stanza has a refrain, which is slightly varied in each verse, and which makes the poem peculiarly difficult to read aloud.

But the deadly hate of Helen burning like a flame, the madness born of poisoned love, the raging passion glowing beneath her stony despair, brought out in contrast with the innocent talk of the child, who watches the terrible drama with the unshrinking interest of childhood, make the poem one of the most exciting, to use a simple word, that can be conceived; and over

[1] There was an edition partly modified and separately edited for the English market.

[2] They will be found carefully collated in Mr. William Sharp's study, *Dante Gabriel Rossetti*, p. 359, etc.

it all broods a deadly fear, which culminates in the final stanza in a breathless horror.

There is no prelude; we are plunged at once, by a simple question of the child, in the very thick of the action :—

> " ' Why did you melt your waxen man,
> Sister Helen?
> To-day is the third since you began.'
> ' The time was long, yet the time ran,
> Little brother.'
> (O Mother, Mary Mother,
> Three days to-day, between Hell and Heaven !) "

Slowly the terrible drama progresses. Helen, worn with despair and rage, sinks on the floor, and the child mounts to the balcony, where the moon flies through broken clouds. The brothers of the dying man come and beg to speak with Helen, and tell the boy of their brother's agony; he no longer prays to live, only to depart. Then the old Baron himself, Keith of Keith, comes—

> " ' He cries to you, kneeling in the road,
> Sister Helen,
> To go with him for the love of God !'
> ' The way is long to his son's abode,
> Little brother.' "

Then the sad bride herself comes; and at last, realising the relentless doom, all ride away; the last drops of wax hiss in the fire, and the flames rise; the soul is free :—

> " ' Ah ! what white thing at the door has cross'd,
> Sister Helen?
> Ah ! what is this that sighs in the frost ?'

'A soul that's lost as mine is lost,
    Little brother!'
            (O Mother, Mary Mother,
Lost, lost, all lost, between Hell and Heaven!)"

I believe that *Rose Mary* may be regarded, not perhaps as the best of Rossetti's writings, but as the most characteristic. In this ballad are blended all the strains that were most potent in his mind. The setting is purely romantic, there is the passion of erring and slighted love, and the whole poem is dominated by the deepest and most mystical supernaturalism. Rossetti's attitude towards the supernatural can be simply defined. He did not, I suppose, believe in the reality of it, in the sense that he expected to encounter it habitually in real life—though in his disordered moods there are hints that he believed himself to be directly in the presence of strange spiritual forces. Neither did he, probably, trouble his head about whether such agencies had in the past ever actually been at work. But the supernatural was, so to speak, an article of his imaginative creed; the conception of it affected him profoundly, and he had an almost childlike relish for supernatural situations. The result was that he wrote of such things not half shamefacedly or ingeniously, but simply and with a kind of direct conviction, which is the essence of sincere art.

The scheme of the poem is this: the maiden Rose Mary is betrothed to Sir James of Heronhaye, and with her mother is awaiting his coming. He is to ride to Holy Cross Abbey at break of day, to be absolved for past sins before the wedding takes place; but he is menaced, the mother knows, by some obscure and deadly peril; an ambush is to be laid for him. In the castle is a mystical stone, the Beryl, in which pure eyes can read what is to be. Mother and daughter consult the stone, and Rose Mary sees the landscape, through which Sir James is to pass, winding before her, while with her eyes she searches it for the ambush. In a stanza of extraordinary vividness she sees spearmen hidden by the floodgates of a ruined weir, among whom is the Warden of Holycleugh. The mother, fearing further peril, makes the girl explore the hillside above, cleft after cleft of the great hill-folds. One of these is brimmed with mist, but there is no trace of any visible ambush there.

In the second part, the mother has divined the secret, that her daughter is not the pure maiden she believed, but has yielded herself to Sir James. Then the mother breaks to her the dreadful news, that looking thus in the Beryl, without the purity of heart that would have disclosed the truth, she has been misled; that the ambush was hidden in the hollow filled with mist, and that Sir James has been borne home dead. Rose Mary falls into a swoon, and the mother goes to the room where the dead man lies, and there on his heart finds a bloodstained packet, with a paper and a lock of hair, from Jocelind, the sister of Holycleugh; and learning that Sir James had not even been true to her whom he has betrayed, she spurns the dead in a passion of rage.

In the third part a cloud has fallen on Rose Mary's mind; she wanders restlessly about the castle, and finds the secret way to the vaulted chapel where the gem is kept; she finds it, and in an access of despair, she cleaves the Beryl with her father's sword. The spirits of the stone fly forth, and Rose Mary dies.

At the end of each part comes a curious lyrical outburst, called the Beryl-songs, the chant of the imprisoned spirits, which are intended to weld the poem together and to supply connections. It is said that Mr. Watts-Dunton, when he first read the poem in proof, said to Rossetti that the drift was too intricate for an ordinary reader. Rossetti took this to heart, and wrote the Beryl-songs to bridge the gaps: Mr. Watts-Dunton, on being shown them, very rightly disapproved, and said humorously that they turned a fine ballad into a bastard opera. Rossetti, who was ill at the time, was so much disconcerted and upset at the criticism, that Mr. Watts-Dunton modified his judgment, and the interludes were printed. But at a later date Rossetti himself came round to the opinion that they were inappropriate. They are curiously wrought, rhapsodical, irregular songs, with fantastic rhymes, and were better away.

But the poem itself has a peculiar colour and charm, as of forms seen through the clear waters of a pool. There is an air of fallen light and dim richness over all. The rhyme scheme is simple: each stanza is a couplet followed by a triplet of rhymes, and the quadruple beat is varied by dactylic and anapaestic movements. It opens thus —

> "'Mary mine that art Mary's Rose,
> Come in to me from the garden-close.
> The sun sinks fast with the rising dew,
> And we marked not how the faint moon grew;
> But the hidden stars are calling you.'"

When the Beryl is replaced in its wrappings, the wizard music, which heralded its disclosure, again comes upon the air :—

"As the globe slid to its silken gloom,
Once more a music rained through the room;
Low it splashed like a sweet star-spray,
And sobbed like tears at the heart of May,
And died as laughter dies away."

I have never been able to feel that either *The White Ship* or *The King's Tragedy* has the peculiar quality of Rossetti's work. Of the latter, Pater says: "Perhaps, if one had to name a single composition of Rossetti's to a reader who desired to make acquaintance with him for the first time, it is *The King's Tragedy* one would select—that poem so moving, so popularly dramatic and lifelike." This may be the case to a certain extent, and it is true that it is a fine historical ballad. "It is a ripper, I can tell you!" wrote Rossetti of it characteristically to Mr. Hall Caine; and he also told Mr. Gosse that he meant it to be one of a series of "extended ballads" from Scottish history; but he wrote no more.

The subject is the murder of King James the First of Scotland, when, in order to save him from the conspirators in the Black Friars' monastery at Perth, Catherine Douglas thrust her arm through the door-staples, to keep the murderers out. The door was forced in, Catherine falling back with a shattered arm, and the king was murdered in the hiding-place in which he had taken refuge. In honour of her deed she received the name of Kate Barlass. She, in her age, is supposed to relate the story; but though there are many beautiful lines and images in the poem, there is also a preponderance of conscientiously historical, but—may it be hinted—dull stanzas. It is, of course, a matter of opinion; but one feels that Rossetti was fettered by facts, and one misses the radiant and mysterious working of imagination which was the mark of the real Rossetti. Some lines, moreover, are introduced to give verisimilitude out of James's own poem *The King's Quhair*, which are clipped down from ten-syllabled lines into eight-syllabled couplets to suit the metre of the poem.

The same lack of individuality is the case in an even more marked degree with *The White Ship*. The ballad was begun in 1877 and finished in 1880, and suffers from a certain dryness and meagreness both of conception and execution, which deprive the work of its characteristic flavour.

The story is the familiar one of the loss of Prince William, the son of Henry I., in the *White Ship*. Henry I. had crossed to Normandy to secure the allegiance of the Norman barons, and was returning in triumph. The *White Ship*, commanded by Fitz-Stephen, the royal hereditary pilot, started after the rest of the fleet; the vessel sank in mid-channel, and all on board were drowned, except Berold, the butcher of Rouen, who tells the tale.

The Bride's Prelude, never finished, belongs to the early period, being written about 1848 or 1849, when Rossetti showed it to William Bell Scott. It was not published till 1881. The original alternative title was *Bridechamber Talk*. It represents the maiden Aloÿse sitting with her sister Amelotte, on a day of heavy summer heat. Aloÿse, very sick at heart, is being attired for her wedding. She lifts her head suddenly—

"'Sister,' said Aloÿse, 'I had
A thing to tell thee of
Long since, and could not.'"

She bids Amelotte pray, and then begins the story of her shame, by first uttering the name of her bridegroom that is to be, Urscelyn. She tells of her sad and timid childhood, how she was one day forced to ride with her brothers, fell, and was carried back to the house. Urscelyn, a young squire, a kinsman of her own, who has some skill in medicine, is summoned to attend her. He learns to desire her, tells his love, and at last she yields herself to him. The sense of her shame grows upon her; but the castle is attacked and burned, and the court have to fly. Urscelyn in the hour of their need deserts them. Aloÿse escapes with her father and brothers to a place of safety, openly avowing her own shame. Her child is born and taken from her; they recover their lands, and Urscelyn comes back. At this point the poem ends, and was never finished, though the scheme of the poem was quite complete in Rossetti's mind,—and indeed his own rough sketch of the plot is preserved.

The charm of the poem is not in the dramatic situation. It is undoubtedly true that the progress is too slow, and that there is a certain strain about the mood. In reading it, the consuming agony of Aloÿse and the sense of the hot and sultry day become almost intolerable. One longs alike for a breath of hope to cool the anguished heart of the bride, and for a fresh wind to cool the fever of the sun.

The beauty of the poem lies rather in the fine dramatic episodes which occur in the course of it, as in the card-playing scene where the girl's shame is symbolised, or the scene where the father strikes down the sword which the brother turns against Aloÿse's breast.

Moreover the workmanship and the detail are throughout of the most delicate; the detail is rich and yet simple, like the careful accessories of a picture. The metre is curious: the first and second lines have no corresponding rhyme, and this is followed by a triplet which has the same rhyme—in places this gives the poem a prosaic effect.

But the poem seems rather like a secret treasury of beautiful things, heaped up in careful profusion, than a tale that is told. No work of Rossetti's is more typical of the Pre-Raphaelite spirit; but the central theme is lost among the wealth of detail lavished upon it.

Such stanzas as the following are wrought like a tapestry:—

> "Although the lattice had dropped loose,
>   There was no wind; the heat
> Being so at rest that Amelotte
> Heard far beneath the plunge and float
> Of a hound swimming in the moat.
>
> Some minutes since, two rooks had toiled
>   Home to the nests that crowned
> Ancestral ash-trees. Through the glare
> Beating again, they seemed to tear
> With that thick caw the woof o' the air.
>
> But else, 'twas at the dead of noon
>   Absolute silence; all,
> From the raised bridge and guarded sconce
> To green-clad places of pleasaunce
> Where the long lake was white with swans."

The Staff and Scrip was written about 1852, and has all the fine freshness of the earlier work. It was published in 1856 in the *Oxford and Cambridge Magazine*. Canon Dixon, who may, however, have been biassed by his association with the poet at the time of its publication, considered it "the finest of all Rossetti's poems, and one of the most glorious writings in the language. It exhibits," he adds, "in flawless perfection the gift that he had above all other writers —absolute beauty and pure action." The idea is taken from the *Gesta Romanorum*, and it is the story of a pilgrim who for love of Queen Blanchelys undertakes to meet in fight Duke Luke, who has burned and harried her lands. He arms himself with armour given by the queen, and leaves his staff and scrip with her. He is slain and brought back dead, and she hangs the staff and scrip over her bed for years, until she dies, waiting to meet him in triumph in heaven.

This poem has the fine *naiveté* and directness, together with a certain stiff stateliness of phrase that Rossetti lost or discarded in his later work.

What could be more delicate than the following?—

> "The Queen sat idle by her loom:
> She heard the arras stir,
> And looked up sadly: through the room
> The sweetness sickened her
> Of musk and myrrh."

And again after the battle, when she takes the staff and scrip—

> "That night they hung above her bed,
> Till morning wet with tears.
> Year after year above her head
> Her bed his token wears,
> Five years, ten years."

And the close has a pure nobility which ends like a solemn music:—

> "Not tithed with days' and years' decease
> He pays thy wage He owed,
> But with imperishable peace
> Here in His own abode,
> Thy jealous God."

Troy Town was written in 1869, and was for a time one of Rossetti's own favourite poems; but there is an excess of sensuous expression throughout. It represents Helen praying at the shrine of Venus. Venus smiles to see that her work is so well done, and Cupid looses an arrow from his string that strikes the heart of Paris, and with the following stanza the poem closes:—

> "Paris turned upon his bed,
> (*O Troy Town!*)
> Turned upon his bed and said,
> Dead at heart with the heart's desire—
> 'Oh to clasp her golden head!'
> (*O Troy's down,
> Tall Troy's on fire!*)"

Eden Bower, which Rossetti called "a splendid subject," was written shortly after *Troy Town*. The subject is the legend of Lilith, once a snake herself, and, after the creation of Adam, turned into a woman, and beloved by him. But she has been first the mate of the serpent of evil, and in a passionate jealousy of the nobler happiness of Adam with his human partner, and enraged at her own expulsion from Paradise, she appeals, in some bewitched grove outside Eden, to the Serpent, to help her in her revenge; to allow her to assume his form for an hour that she may tempt and destroy the happy pair. She exults over the success which she foresees, over all the misery which will ensue, and over the joy with which she will return to her first mate. She sings—

> "'O but Adam was thrall to Lilith!
> (*Alas the hour!*)
> All the threads of my hair are golden,
> And there in a net his heart was holden.'"

But here again there is a certain baseness of physical horror at the idea, which is dwelt on throughout the poem, of the embrace of the snake. The ψυχρὸς ὄφις has an instinctive repulsion for humanity, which poisons the beauty of the poem at its source.

Stratton Water, as has been said, is an almost purely archaic revival. Rossetti considered it "successful only in so far as any imitation of the old ballad can be successful," but, within this degree, he believed it to be as good as anything of the kind by any living writer. It was much altered from its original draft.

The story is of a maiden, Janet, who has given herself to Lord Sands, and goes out, wild with despair, to drown herself in the flooded Stratton Water. Lord Sands has been led to believe her dead, but meets her on the edge of the stream, catches a floating boat, rows her to the church, where they are married, and home for her child to be born.

To turn to the principal lyrics: in considering the poem of the *Blessed Damozel*, the thought that the poem was written in early youth must always be attended by a certain wonder. It seems probable that Rossetti had the poem in his mind when he once wrote that a writer must often do some of his best work at an early age, and find it out later in a rage. The poem has all the freshness of youth, the delight that attends the radiant spirit, nursed in dreams of beauty, when it finds that it too can achieve, and feels the thrill and stir of the lute-strings answering faithfully the timid and adoring touch. Though at first sight the delicate archaic handling of language is a great attraction, yet it is the combination of vastness and nearness in the poem which lends it an incomparable charm. We find ourselves rapt into a far-off aërial distance—

> "Beneath, the tides of day and night
>   With flame and darkness ridge
> The void, as low as where this earth
>   Spins like a fretful midge."

The daring of this touch, the directness so characteristic of the Pre-Raphaelite idea, the almost meanness of the comparison, is only justified by the sense of immensity that it lends—

> "From the fixed place of Heaven she saw
>   Time like a pulse shake fierce
> Through all the worlds."

But then, in contrast to the depth and distance of the picture, comes the thought of the nearness and closeness of the tie of human love, that passes through the dizzy spaces like an electric thrill, and holds the longing, faithful hearts close together, even though one stands in the tranquil and serene fortress of heaven, and the other spins, a fevered mortal atom, in the poor, fretful world. There is the gentle faith in the far-off union, the passionate heart forecasting the perfect happiness of the meeting. "'For he will come,' she said."

Another daring and exquisite device is the interjecting at intervals, in language of perfect simplicity and yet without the archaism of the main poem, the thoughts of the distant lover, still enchained by earth—

> "(Ah sweet! Even now, in that bird's song,
>   Strove not her accents there,
> Fain to be hearkened? When those bells
>   Possessed the mid-day air,
> Strove not her steps to reach my side
>   Down all the echoing stair?)"

The delicate quaintness of the poem is in itself a charm, though it is strained to its utmost limits in the verse that tells the names of the five handmaidens of Mary, or the angels with "their citherns and citoles"; but even here the informing spirit of the whole is present, and there is no sense of literary ornament. They are only the sweet accessories, told as a child might tell them, of a definite scene.

There is no need to trace the genesis of the poem, for indeed it owes little to any previous writer; but I have sometimes thought that the *Ancient Mariner* was the germ of the treatment, though with little affinity of thought. There is a distant echo of Coleridge in the stanza—

> "The sun was gone now; the curled moon
>   Was like a little feather
> Fluttering far down the gulf; and now
>   She spoke through the still weather."

The poem was constantly retouched. The beautiful lines in the first stanza—

> "Her eyes were deeper than the depth
>   Of waters stilled at even"

ran originally—

> "Her blue grave eyes were deeper much
> Than a deep water even"

and passed through an intermediate stage, in the *Oxford and Cambridge Magazine*, as—

> "Her eyes knew more of rest and shade
> Than waters stilled at even."

In the fourteenth stanza—

> "And see our old prayers, granted, melt
> Each like a little cloud"

originally ran, in the *Germ*—

> "And where each need, revealed, expects
> Its patient period."

But the most interesting series of alterations will be found in stanza seven—

> "Around her, lovers, newly met
>   'Mid deathless love's acclaims,
> Spoke evermore among themselves
>   Their heart-remembered names."

The second line is not wholly satisfactory, because it is not quite clear whether the praise of deathless love or the praises uttered by lovers who have passed into life is meant. In the *Germ* it ran—

> "Heard hardly, some of her new friends
>   Playing at holy games,
> Spake, gentle-mouthed among themselves
>   Their virginal new names"

and it passed through two separate stages before it reached its final form.

So stands this beautiful poem, a supreme instance

of the charging of an ancient form with the most passionate dreams of to-day.[1]

The poem of *Jenny* stands alone among Rossetti's poems as *Found* among his pictures. It gives us the regretful feeling that Rossetti's art did not reach its full and free development. It is a piece of the very stuff of life; it is water drawn from life's deepest and bitterest well, and presented in a chalice of pure gold. It is far beyond any sermon, for it is the thing itself, the saddest thing that the world can hold. The nearest approach to a moral is in the concluding lines—

> "Well, of such thoughts so much I know :
> In my life, as in hers, they show,
> By a far gleam which I may near,
> A dark path I can strive to clear."

The poem is put in the mouth of one who has lived a careless life in his youth, but has found his work in the world—it is hinted that he is a student. One evening he has a sudden impulse toward the old and half-forgotten days of so-called pleasure; he meets at some dancing-hall a girl, whose fallen life has not as yet dimmed her childish beauty, and accompanies her home. There she falls asleep with her head on his knee; he does not wake her, but muses over what she was, is, and will be : there comes into his mind the thought of a girl, a young cousin of his, whose nature is as thoughtless and pleasure-loving, but who is sheltered by circumstances, and for whom waits a happy and unsullied love. The wonder, the hopeless

---

[1] The alterations in the text are well worth careful study. They are conveniently and carefully summarised by Mr. William Sharp on pp. 339, 340 of his *Dante Gabriel Rossetti*.

and bewildering riddle of why such things should become before him: why evil should set its mark upon one of the lilies of the garden of life and not upon another, and what restoration is possible—

> "What lullaby
> Of sweet forgetful second birth
> Remains? All dark. No sign on earth
> What measure of God's rest endows
> The many mansions of His house."

Jenny is a plaything; she does not understand what is happening, and she drifts along taking such pleasure as comes in her way, dancing into the shadow of death.

The problem is only stated; no solution is attempted, no far-off hope shines beyond the dark cloud. Only once or twice a certain scorn breaks out, which may be held to detract from the solemn mood, as in the passage describing the vesting of Priapus to seem

> "An eligible deity,"

and there is a grim paronomasia,

> "Whose *person* or whose *purse* may be
> The lodestar of your reverie."

The pathos has been sometimes held to be a literary pathos, but that is a wholly unjust view. The sad truth in all its bearings is seen with the hard lucidity of vision of which Rossetti had the secret; and the fact that the enigma seems insoluble does not argue any want of emotion; it is simply cast down before the heart with a gesture of despair—

> "How atone,
> Great God, for this which man has done?"

But of course the form is here the supreme thing.

The problem is as old as life and time; but to state it without affectation, without morbidity, without mawkishness, in words of flawless beauty and exquisite dignity, is what places the poem among the high achievements of art. What could be more absolutely arresting than the contrast between Jenny's childish thought of the great town and the reality?—

> "Haply at times a passing thought
> Of the old days which seem to be
> Much older than any history
> That is written in any book;
> When she would lie in fields and look
> Along the ground through the blown grass,
> And wonder where the city was,
> Far out of sight, whose broil and bale
> They told her then for a child's tale.
>
> Jenny, you know the city now."

The last line of the above, in its simplicity, is pathos at white heat, the very essence of the world's sorrow distilled.

Again, what could be truer than the image of the

> "Rose shut in a book
> In which pure women may not look.
>
> . . . . .
>
> Yet still it keeps such faded show
> Of when 'twas gathered long ago,
> That the crushed petals' lovely grain,
> The sweetness of the sanguine stain,
> Seen of a woman's eyes, must make
> Her pitiful heart, so prone to ache,
> Love roses better for its sake."

The last line speaks of a divine pity more than can be asked of human nature.

And again, what could be nobler than the rhetoric of the image of Lust?—

> "Like a toad within a stone
> Seated while Time crumbles on ;
> Which sits there since the earth was curs'd
> For Man's transgression at the first ;
> Which, living through all centuries,
> Not once has seen the sun arise ;
> Whose life, to its cold circle charmed,
> The earth's whole summers have not warmed ;
> Which always—whitherso the stone
> Be flung—sits there, deaf, blind, alone ;—
> Aye, and shall not be driven out
> Till that which shuts him round about
> Break at the very Master's stroke,
> And the dust thereof vanish as smoke,
> And the seed of Man vanish as dust :—
> Even so within this world is Lust."

It is difficult to estimate the worth of a contemporary poem, most of all a poem that is in no sense written *virginibus puerisque*. But apart from hysterical imagination, it is hard to believe that *Jenny* is not one of the monumental poems of the century that gave it birth.

The history of the poem demands a few words. Rossetti's own account was as follows ;—"*Jenny* (in a first form) was written almost as early as *The Blessed Damozel*, which I wrote (and have altered little since), when I was eighteen. It was first printed when I was twenty-one. Of the first *Jenny*, perhaps fifty lines survive here and there, but I felt it was quite beyond me then (a world I was then happy enough to be a stranger to), and later I re-wrote it completely."

The early draft is still in existence. It contains some

of the later lines, but is characterised by a directness, almost coarseness, which is in strong contrast to the completed poem.

One word should be said about the metre. It is of course the simplest iambic couplet, with here and there a third line added; but out of this not very dignified metre, by a skilful shifting of stress, never degenerating into any metrical trick, a great variety of effects are produced. The couplet is as a rule divided at the end of a paragraph, so as to link in an informal way one strophe with the next, by keeping the ear unsatisfied. There is an extraordinary command of emphasis throughout. Such lines as

"The many aims or the few years"

and

"Much older than any history"

and

"And the dust thereof vanish as smoke"

are almost perfect instances of an instinct for compensation in weight of sound. No rules could produce such lines; they are the flower of instinctive skill.

Dante at Verona is an early poem, a very carefully studied picture of Dante's life in exile, in the house of Can Grande della Scala. It is difficult exactly to describe it. It is some five hundred lines long, and is an elaborate description of the bitter life of exile, the humiliation, the loneliness, the upholding visions and the unconscious dignity of the life lived among such despondent conditions. The legend is very skilfully intertwined, but it is difficult not to feel that the subject is overweighted, though the poem is full of memorable stanzas and stately lines. It has little of the *naïveté* of most of Rossetti's early work, but is a deliberate and balanced piece of craftsmanship; one feels the swift heart-beats of anger under the vigorous, masculine lines; the whole poem has a suppressed passion, a noble scorn for the petty agitations that made such a life possible. Shall not Florence, he says, yet make amends?—

> "O God! or shall dead souls deny
> The undying soul its prophecy?
>
> Aye, 'tis their hour."

So he moves, half sick at heart in an alien land, half intent on the fair vision in his soul. He is utterly indifferent to all the bright life around him, the feasting and the jesting, until his presence becomes "a peevish sufferance." He scorns the offer that comes from Florence of pardon to the exiles, if they will submit to fine and penance. Yet he keeps his other task in mind, to write worthily—

> "Yea even of her; no rhymes uncouth
> 'Twixt tongue and tongue; but by God's aid
> The first words Italy had said."

And so he achieves the dream, though in sadness unutterable; till at last he turns his back upon the court that has become hateful to him, and goes out into the world again. But even Rossetti's art, thus intently applied, fails to make the subject wholly attractive. There is something ungenerous in Dante's scornful acceptance of hospitality, and his undisguised contempt for his entertainers, which remains more curmudgeonly than magnificent, in spite of all that can be said to make it seem natural or noble.

A Last Confession is a story of tragic love, dramatically conceived and limpidly expressed. The incidents are kept very prominently in the foreground. All the surroundings are studied with great veracity. It is a story of troubled times, when a volunteer in the cause of liberty in the struggle between Austria and Italy, living a hunted life, finds and takes charge of an orphan child, who becomes the delight and solace of his life. He finds that his paternal and protective love gradually ripens into a passionate devotion ; while the simple and affectionate child meanwhile develops into a hard and sensual woman, and laughs at him and his proffered gift. In a moment which is half madness and half passionate impulse to save her from degradation, he stabs her to the heart. He tells the tale as he lies, long after, dying of wounds received in fight.

It is a fine story, finely told. The simplicity of the pure and tender-hearted patriot is very subtly developed. But it is not a characteristic poem, though it shows, like other poems of the early time, the veins, so to speak, of unworked ore, and the mastery Rossetti might have achieved in dramatic narrative if he had developed it more diligently.

The following extract may be quoted :—

"For now, being always with her, the first love
I had—the father's, brother's love—was changed,
I think, in somewise ; like a holy thought
Which is a prayer before one knows of it.
The first time I perceived this, I remember,
Was once when after hunting I came home
Weary, and she brought food and fruit for me,
And sat down at my feet upon the floor
Leaning against my side. But when I felt
Her sweet head reach from that low seat of hers

> So high as to be laid upon my heart,
> I turned and looked upon my darling there
> And marked for the first time how tall she was;
> And my heart beat with so much violence
> Under her cheek, I thought she could not choose
> But wonder at it soon and ask me why;
> And so I bade her rise and eat with me.
> And when, remembering all and counting back
> The time, I made out fourteen years for her
> And told her so, she gazed at me with eyes
> As of the sky and sea on a grey day,
> And drew her long hands through her hair, and
>   asked me
> If she was not a woman; and then laughed:
> And as she stooped in laughing, I could see
> Beneath the growing throat the breasts half-globed
> Like folded lilies deepset in the stream."

The Portrait, which is one of the earliest works, and which, as has been pointed out, shows a certain trace of Tennyson's influence, will hold its place as one of the finest, if not the finest, of the strong and solid poems that show how Rossetti might have developed in the direction of simple stateliness:—

> "This is her picture as she was:
>   It seems a thing to wonder on,
>   As though mine image in the glass
>   Should tarry when myself am gone.
>   I gaze until she seems to stir,—
>   Until mine eyes almost aver
>   That now, even now, the sweet lips part
>   To breathe the words of the sweet heart:—
>   And yet the earth is over her.
>
>   Alas! even such the thin-drawn ray
>   That makes the prison-depths more rude,—
>   The drip of water night and day
>   Giving a tongue to solitude.

> Yet only this, of love's whole prize,
> Remains ; save what in mournful guise
>   Takes counsel with my soul alone,—
>   Save what is secret and unknown,
> Below the earth, above the skies."

The natural touches in the poem are conceived with perfect simplicity—

> "When the leaf-shadows at a breath
> Shrink in the road, and all the heath,
>   Forest and water, far and wide,
>   In limpid starlight glorified,
> Lie like the mystery of death."

If I had to select one poem of Rossetti's to illustrate the early simple manner at its very best, I should certainly choose *The Portrait*. Here is nothing voluptuous, nothing extravagant. Stanza by stanza the sweet music goes its way, rising at the end into a tender and divine close.

The *Ave* is another of these austere and restrained poems, like a strain of religious music. He adopts Catholic dogma, and places the Blessed Virgin on the very throne of heaven—

> "Oh when our need is uttermost,
>   Think that to such as death may strike
>   Thou once wert sister sisterlike ! "

The description of the Annunciation Day is very tenderly drawn—

> "Mind'st thou not (when June's heavy breath
> Warmed the long days in Nazareth,)
> That eve thou didst go forth to give
> Thy flowers some drink that they might live
> One faint night more amid the sands ?
> Far off the trees were as pale wands

> Against the fervid sky : the sea
> Sighed further off eternally
> As human sorrow sighs in sleep.
> Then suddenly the awe grew deep,
> As of a day to which all days
> Were footsteps in God's secret ways :
> Until a folding sense, like prayer,
> Which is, as God is, everywhere,
> Gathered about thee ; and a voice
> Spake to thee without any noise,
> Being of the silence :—' Hail,' it said,
> ' Thou that art highly favourèd ;
> The Lord is with thee here and now ;
> Blessed among all women thou.'"

And again—

> " Mind'st thou not (when the twilight gone
> Left darkness in the house of John,)
> Between the naked window-bars
> That spacious vigil of the stars ?"

The whole poem has an exquisite progress, like a flowing stream.

The Burden of Nineveh was written about 1850. It appeared in its original form in the *Oxford and Cambridge Magazine*. Ruskin on reading it wrote to Rossetti: "I am wild to know who is the author of *The Burden of Nineveh*, in No. 8. . . . It is glorious."

Ruskin's next letter contains the word *Bravo!* written very large and shaped out of notes of admiration, and no doubt refers to Rossetti's avowal of authorship.

The subject is the arrival of a sculptured beast from the excavations at Nineveh at the British Museum, and the thought of all the vicissitudes it has endured.

It is, as it stands, a noble poem full of strong

imagery and allusion, and thrilling with light and sound. Perhaps the finest of many fine stanzas is

> "Oh when upon each sculptured court,
> Where even the wind might not resort,—
> O'er which Time passed, of like import
> With the wild Arab boys at sport,—
> A living face looked in to see :—
> Oh seemed it not—the spell once broke—
> As though the carven warriors woke,
> As though the shaft the string forsook,
> The cymbals clashed, the chariots shook,
> And there was life in Nineveh?"

The metre, as will be seen, is one that imposes a great strain on the invention of rhyme. But there is a splendid *verve* and rush all through, that speaks of a living fountain of imagination and language springing loudly from an echoing spring.

A few of the lyrics may now be considered. First perhaps of all comes *The Stream's Secret*, a long lyric, with a peculiar and delicate music of its own, which has caught the very cadence of water, lapsing and murmuring, with many an eddy, many a backward gush, turning still upon itself, and swayed this way and that, meeting the very obstacles that would stay it with a soft and yielding evasion, and yet speeding resistlessly upon its way. The lyric was for the most part written in a little cave beside the stream, and the very spirit of the flood has passed into these strange and musical lines:—

> "What thing unto mine ear
> Wouldst thou convey,—what secret thing,
> O wandering water ever whispering?
> Surely thy speech shall be of her.
> Thou water, O thou whispering wanderer,
> What message dost thou bring?

> Say, hath not Love leaned low
> This hour beside thy far well-head,
> And there through jealous hollowed fingers said
> The thing that most I long to know?"

It is of Love that he makes question, love that seems to have taken wing—

> "But she is far away
> Now; nor the hours of night grown hoar
> Bring yet to me, long gazing from the door,
> The wind-stirred robe of roseate grey
> And rose-crown of the hour that leads the day
> When we shall meet once more."

The stream flows on, guarding the secret that it seems fain to utter. The stanza in which he speaks the very secret of the heart, his restless imperious quest of love, runs thus:—

> "But hear, before thou speak!
> Withhold, I pray, the vain behest
> That while the maze hath still its bower for quest
> My burning heart should cease to seek.
> Be sure that Love ordained for souls more meek
> His roadside dells of rest."

Another of the poems that seems to hover on the verge of sleep, in a dreamful land, is the beautiful lyric *Insomnia*, with its soft burden—

> "Thin are the night-skirts left behind
> By daybreak hours that onward creep,
> And thin, alas! the shred of sleep
> That wavers with the spirit's wind:
> But in half-dreams that shift and roll
> And still remember and forget,
> My soul this hour has drawn your soul
> A little nearer yet."

One of the lightest and most musical of the lesser lyrics is the beautiful *Love-Lily*, which has a delicate lilt given it by the light rhyme of the word *Love-Lily* which in each stanza ends the second line:—

> "Within the voice, within the heart,
> Within the mind of Love-Lily,
> A spirit is born who lifts apart
> His tremulous wings and looks at me;
> Who on my mouth his finger lays,
> And shows, while whispering lutes confer,
> That Eden of Love's watered ways
> Whose winds and spirits wership her."

But the poem is particularly notable for the gnomic couplet at the end, already quoted, which, more than any other compressed phrase, sums up Rossetti's whole philosophy of love—

> "Whose speech Truth knows not from her thought,
> Nor Love her body from her soul."

It has been rightly said that the title of Rossetti's great sonnet-sequence, *The House of Life*, is too catholic in its import. It is rather the House of Love; but the title is significant, because it shows the place that Love held in Rossetti's philosophy, and proves clearly enough that for him love was the all-embracing secret and mystery of life. It is divided into two sections. The first fifty-nine sonnets are *Youth and Change*; the last, LX.-CI., are *Change and Fate*. The structure varies to a certain extent. The octaves are mostly built on the same scheme of two rhymes (A, B, B, A, A, B, B, A). But the sestettes are varied. Some are constructed out of two rhymes, some of three, arranged in a great diversity of order. This variety of form Rossetti considered to be not only permissible but desirable; he did not consider that what is commonly called the Petrarchan form was at all binding. He once wrote: "The English sonnet *too much* tampered with becomes a sort of bastard madrigal. *Too much, invariably* restricted, it degenerates into a Shibboleth."

The *House of Life* is not constructed on a definite plan: the MSS., which I have carefully studied, bear witness to the perpetual alterations and rearrangements which took place before the eventual publication, and reveal how hard a task it was for Rossetti to satisfy himself. The sequence contains some of his earliest work and some of his latest; but it is in effect a sort of commentary on life as Rossetti conceived it, and there is a certain evolution of experience throughout. It opens in hope and youth; then death strikes sternly through the sweet dream and shatters the vase of life; then the fragments are, so to speak, pieced together in sadness and despair, but the glimmer of hope grows stronger until patience, if not tranquillity, is attained.

This evolution may, however, enable us to trace, in so far as anything so mystical and subtle may be apprehended and stated, Rossetti's own philosophy of life. The creed is enunciated in the first of the sonnets, *Love Enthroned* :—

"I marked all kindred Powers the heart finds fair :—
    Truth, with awed lips ; and Hope, with eyes upcast ;
    And Fame, whose loud wings fan the ashen Past
To signal-fires, Oblivion's flight to scare ;
And Youth, with still some single golden hair
    Unto his shoulder clinging, since the last
    Embrace wherein two sweet arms held him fast ;
And Life, still wreathing flowers for Death to wear.

Love's throne was not with these :"

He sits far apart—

> "Though Truth foreknow Love's heart, and Hope foretell,
> And Fame be for Love's sake desirable,
> And Youth be dear, and Life be sweet to Love."

Love, then, is the supreme secret, lord of all the powers of heart and mind and soul.

This love is inextricably intertwined with beauty. Though it may exist independently, beauty is the actual and visible symbol of the secret. This is clearly stated in lxxvii., *Soul's Beauty* :—

> "Under the arch of Life, where love and death,
> Terror and mystery, guard her shrine, I saw
> Beauty enthroned ; and though her gaze struck awe,
> I drew it in as simply as my breath."

In the light of this secret all things are to be interpreted, and the soul is therethrough, as from a secret window, to look out upon the unknown land.

This love, too, is not a sudden thing, which might or might not have been, depending upon mortal chances of vicinity and time; it is deeper and older, as old as the earth and as deep as the far-off purposes of God (*The Birth-bond*, xv.)—

> "Even so, when first I saw you, seemed it, love,
> That among souls allied to mine was yet
> One nearer kindred than life hinted of.
> O born with me somewhere that men forget,
> And though in years of sight and sound unmet,
> Known for my soul's birth-partner well enough !"

The truth is known in a moment, and perceived by both hearts (*Love-Sweetness*, xxi.)—

> "the swift beat
> And soft subsidence of the spirit's wing,
> Then when it feels, in cloud-girt wayfaring
> The breath of kindred plumes against its feet."

But the lover must not, as the rapture grows, lose sight of his insignificance—

> "Lo! what am I to Love, the lord of all?
>   One murmuring shell he gathers from the sand,—
>   One little heart-flame sheltered in his hand."

Then the shadow falls. The beloved face rises in the spring of Willowwood, rises and sinks again—

> "and if it ever may
> Meet mine again I know not if Love knows."

Then follows *Without Her* (liii.), a sacred poem, drawn from Rossetti in an hour of ghastly solitude, in the days when the hinge of his life turned swiftly. When the passionate sorrow has a little died away, Love gives the singer a glistening leaf, saying (lix.):—

> "Only this laurel dreads no winter days:
> Take my last gift; thy heart hath sung my praise."

Then the mood changes, and the harder, graver experiences of life flow in upon the desolate soul. The spirit counts its treasures up, and garners the worth of life, sometimes hopeful, sometimes sad, whether it sees (lxii.)

> "Visions of golden futures: or that last
>   Wild pageant of the accumulated past
>   That clangs and flashes for a drowning man."

There are dark days (lxviii.)—

> "The gloom that breathes upon me with these airs
>   Is like the drops which strike the traveller's brow
>   Who knows not, darkling, if they bring him now
> Fresh storm, or be old rain the covert bears."

Nature and Art are ransacked for their secrets: but

behind them all flies a dark shadow of mystery for the lonely soul. The spirit grows bewildered, looking back, and wonders what all the strange wanderings signify (lxxx.)—

> " Even so the thought that is at length full grown
> Turns back to note the sun-smit paths, all grey
> And marvellous once, where first it walked alone ;
> And haply doubts, amid the unblenching day,
> Which most or least impelled its onward way,—
> Those unknown things or these things overknown."

There breaks upon the heart the sense that it too must make its farewells and be gone, that the cup is drunk out and the life lived. He turns away from the glen he has loved (lxxxiv.)—

> " And yet, farewell ! For better shalt thou fare
> When children bathe sweet faces in thy flow
> And happy lovers blend sweet shadows there
> In hours to come, than when an hour ago
> Thine echoes had but one man's sighs to bear
> And thy trees whispered what he feared to know."

Remorse for lost days falls upon him. In one of the noblest of the sonnets, regarded by himself as one of his highest achievements, he writes (*Lost Days*, lxxxvi.)—

> " The lost days of my life until to-day,
> What were they, could I see them on the street
> Lie as they fell ? Would they be ears of wheat
> Sown once for food but trodden into clay ?
> Or golden coins squandered and still to pay ?
> Or drops of blood dabbling the guilty feet ?
> Or such spilt water as in dreams must cheat
> The undying throats of Hell, athirst alway ?"

He will see them, he knows, and hear them each speak—

> "'I am thyself,—what hast thou done to me?'
> 'And I—and I—thyself,' (lo! each one saith,)
> 'And thou thyself to all eternity!'"

The spirit cowers in the shadow of death, and (xciii.)

> "Then sends one sigh forth to the unknown goal,
> And bitterly feels breathe against his soul
> The hour swift-winged of nearer nothingness."

The "shaken shadow intolerable" speaks (xcvii.)—

> "'Look in my face; my name is Might-have-been;
> I am also called No-more, Too-late, Farewell.'"

But as the spirit learns its lesson of patience the mood changes (xcix.)—

> "To-day Death seems to me an infant child
> Which her worn mother Life upon my knee
> Has set to grow my friend and play with me."

And then, all at once, like a sad music gathering itself up, and dying on one sweet, solemn, and joyful chord, the *One Hope* steals upon the heart—

> "When vain desire at last and vain regret
>   Go hand in hand to death, and all is vain,
>   What shall assuage the unforgotten pain
> And teach the unforgetful to forget?
>
> . . . . . .
>
> Ah! when the wan soul in that golden air
>   Between the scriptured petals softly blown
>   Peers breathless for the gift of grace unknown,—
> Ah! let none other alien spell soe'er
> But only the one Hope's one name be there,—
>   Not less nor more, but even that word alone."

So closes this strange, sad book of the heart's experience. The impression that it leaves upon the mind and spirit is one that it is difficult even to attempt to analyse. It is wellnigh impossible not to fall under the almost magical spell of the long-drawn, solemn beauty of the words. Of course it is transcendental, spun of light and dew; and for those who admit no further depth in love and life than material rapture, delicate sensations, and sensuous excitement, it is doubtless merely bewildering and over-strained.

It is true that in many of the sonnets there is a certain weary fever of the body, a passionate voluptuousness which offends and must offend the temperate and controlled spirit.

But that is not all; other poets, such as Shakespeare, Milton, Keats, and Browning, have been voluptuous enough without offending. In Rossetti, what offends is a certain softness of execution, but more a want of reserve, which makes him appear at times as if overmastered by a kind of sensuous hysteria. The poets mentioned above have been plain-spoken enough on the subject of love without offending, because they have spoken as it were boldly and unashamedly. But there are moments when one fears, as it were, to catch Rossetti's eye, when there is a lack not only of dignity but of decorum.

Further, it is interesting to contrast this note with the note of self-sacrifice, the deliberate, almost ecstatic, turning of the back on material pleasure that runs so strongly through all his sister Christina's work. In his own, there is a languid surrender to the physical joys of love which seems to have within it a taint, as though love were a spirit bound by laws of beauty only, and nonexistent beside them. But the largeness of the message of love for humanity is that it may triumph completely over all that is voluptuous and seductive, and that in that purer air his wings beat more urgently and radiantly, and lift the soul to a height of nobleness and sacrifice which seems undreamed of in the *House of Life*.

Thus it is that the book has an enervating effect upon the spirit. It seems shuttered close in a fragrant gloom of strange perfumes which have a perilous and magical sweetness about them. But one longs for something more simple and natural, a breath of fresh woods, or the falling of some sharp and cold wave, with brisk and briny savours. One longs to come out into a place of liberty from this fallen light, this hushed and perfumed chamber.

This feeling is heightened, in reading the *House of Life*, by the incorporation of some of the earlier work into the sequence. These more immature sonnets, even when one feels that the mastery of word and technique is less complete, are like spaces of sunlight in a forest. Elaboration and gorgeousness are not inconsistent with freshness of conception; but it is impossible not to feel that there is a certain brightness as of morning light, a temperamental thing, which is absent from some of the most finished structures of Rossetti's later manner. One asks oneself uneasily whether these latter are not rather art than poetry, appealing rather to the mind, and the cultivated sense, than to the primal delight in things of beauty, rapturously and suddenly apprehended. The impressions are not clearly and freshly seen, but veil themselves dimly under heavy ornate fabrics, beneath which the outline tends to disappear. The initial impulse seems weaker, the outlook more conventional. Magnificence of manner has taken the place of a wondering delight.

Still, as a literary work it is a treasure-house of incomparable richness. The splendour of the noble, resonant lines, the music of the slow-moving verse, the stateliness of conception, the perfect progression and balance of sonnet after sonnet—all these are there. Many of these noble phrases dwell and re-echo in the mind. Yet I would say that there must be a certain sense of revolt against the overpowering seductiveness of thought and music; they are like the song of the sirens above the bone-strewn strand, and can only be safely heard by the wary, much-enduring hero, with limbs bound close to the mast. Or they are as the enchanted house of Circe, and may be gazed upon with delight and fearless joy, if only the gazer carry the holy herb in his bosom, against which the magical spells beat in vain.

Of the sonnets outside the *House of Life* there are three distinct classes:—The early sonnets in the Pre-Raphaelite manner; Sonnets in the later manner; Literary sonnets, which form a class apart; and apart from these stand two sonnets, *Winter* and *Spring*, which are beautiful transcripts of Nature.

The early sonnets are among the most beautiful of Rossetti's work. To these belong *A Venetian Pastoral*, discussed elsewhere. This was much strengthened and improved at a later date. *Mary's Girlhood*, which is characterised by the most perfect and daring simplicity; such lines as—

> "Unto God's will she brought devout respect,
> Profound simplicity of intellect,
>   And supreme patience"

apart from their setting, seem almost too naive for art; but Rossetti never wrote sweeter lines than—

> "An angel-watered lily, that near God
> Grows and is quiet."

Of the second class are such careful sonnets as *Venus Verticordia* and *Pandora*; but such phrases in the latter as "the Olympian consistory" and

> "Powers of the impassioned hours prohibited,"

are instances of Rossetti's instinct to carry linguistic elaboration beyond the bounds of beauty.

Of the third class,—the literary sonnets,—those on Chatterton and Shelley seem almost too rhetorical; yet they show a great intellectual skill in seizing salient points. Those on Coleridge and Keats are majestic, especially the end of the latter.

> "thy name, not writ
> But rumour'd in water, while the fame of it
> Along Time's flood goes echoing evermore,"

has a wonderful liquid beat, very close to the image it employs.

The two nature-sonnets, *Spring* and *Winter*, are both delicate pieces of observation, and show what Rossetti might have done in this manner had he had more such material to work upon. Such a line as

> "The young rooks cheep 'mid the thick caw o' the old,"

is a microscopic touch of tender observation.

And again, in the *Winter* sonnet:—

"How large that thrush looks on the bare thorn-tree!
A swarm of such, three little months ago,
Had hidden in the leaves and let none know
Save by the outburst of their minstrelsy."

The more that we consider where Rossetti stands in relation to the literature of the century, the more lonely and esoteric his position will appear. We shall feel that he stands like a tree transplanted from some foreign soil, which though by some happy accident of soil and air and sun it shot out great branched glories, soft layers of shade, yet remains essentially exotic, a tree, so to speak, of a pleasaunce, with no congruity with the wild harmony of the native woodland. Compare him with Shelley, Coleridge, Wordsworth, Scott, and Byron; with Keats, Clough, Browning, Arnold, and Tennyson—the great names of the era. With the casuistical melancholy of Clough and his broken cadences he has no affinity at all, and hardly more with the Greek purity, the austere restraint of Arnold. With Browning he had more in common; yet the kinship is but a superficial thing. Indeed if the circumstances of the lives of the two poets were detailed and the works of the pair were put unnamed into the hands of a critical reader, he would probably think that he detected in Browning's hankering instinct after Italy and Southern skies the home-sickness of a Neapolitan for the land of his forefathers; while in Rossetti's ballads he might trace an ancestral attachment to the romance of the Celt, to moorland country with its babbling streams overlooked from a grey castle keep. There is no deep resemblance between the two; indeed, the catholicity of Browning's humanity, the zest for touching, tasting, and feeling life at all points, the irresistible desire to see every one's point of view from the inside, is the strongest contrast that can be conceived to Rossetti's deliberate selection of certain experiences, and his jealous exclusion of all phenomena that did not march with his taste.

With Tennyson there is a nearer bond, for Tennyson, like Rossetti, tended to live in a world of his own devising; and there are certain of Tennyson's poems that bear a decided affinity to the work of Rossetti. There is the fidelity to detail, the strong power of realising pictorially the romantic surroundings of a scene; both, too, have the power of vividly presenting a situation from a single point of view, and the weakness in grasping the dramatic significance of the interplay of varied character. But Tennyson has more catholicity, more serenity, more philosophical curiosity; he had an intense desire to solve the riddle of the "painful earth," while Rossetti had an overpowering desire to escape from it into the region of immediate sensation.

Rossetti had none of the impulse "to see life steadily and to see it whole"; he rather desired to live in the intensity of the instant, to lose himself in the emotional crisis, the beautiful adjuncts of the picture.

To pass, then, from his contemporaries to the earlier names of the century. Scott would have appeared to Rossetti, in poetry, a mere loose narrator, lost in the childish pleasure of a tale, but without concentration, and without the ecstatic sense of sudden beauty. Wordsworth seemed to him a rustical proser, without dignity of conception or execution; Byron a gifted amateur. In Shelley he found a superabundance of unreal philanthropy, and a lyrical beauty which came, as it were, by a rhapsodical impulse, without sustained intention and without artistic devotion.

There remain the names of Coleridge and Keats, to whom in spiritual ancestry Rossetti was the nearest. In Coleridge he saw a genius overpowered by indolence and vapid philosophy; but the *Ancient Mariner* and *Christabel* had no doubt a directly inspiring effect upon Rossetti's mode of conception and execution. In these poems there is the same romantic isolation; their scene is laid beyond the faery casement, on the perilous seas forlorn, and in the enchanted woodland of the land of dreams. To Keats Rossetti owed a true allegiance: there is the same richness of fancy, the same voluptuousness of mood, the same deliberate intention of wringing beauty out of the moment and the scene. But Keats is a truer because a larger poet; and there are regions into which Rossetti could rarely follow him, where Keats came face to face with the pathos of the world, and saw that it was good; where he saw without rebellion, and in the higher, more prophetic mood, the sadness of all sweet things that have an end.

It is in this absence of detachment that Rossetti goes nearest to forfeiting his claim to be considered a poet of the first rank. There is a haunting sense of the desire of possession about much of his poetry, particularly in the later years. From his best work it is absent; but only in his best work does one lose sight of the personality of the poet; and if his perception of beauty had not been so acute, and his power of expression so magical, it would have had the effect of marring much of his work.

If he stands apart from his predecessors, so does he

stand apart from his successors. He cannot be said to have modified in any direct way the great stream of English poetry. The poets whom he profoundly affected have been of a secondary order, poets who have been more concerned with the manner than the matter of their verse.

Indeed, we can easily imagine that a man of high poetical impulse would tend to shun the writings of Rossetti rather than become familiar with them, just as his friends tended to draw apart in a spirit of revolt from the mental domination of the man. So it was that Stevenson, we are told, would not read Livy, and Pater would not read Stevenson, because of the consciousness that these contagious stylists tended to draw them away from their own mode of expression in a kind of insensible imitation.

Thus with Rossetti, his effects are so gorgeous, so individual, so definitely mannerised; the technical perfection is so supreme, that it is difficult, if one falls under the spell of Rossetti, not to follow in the track of what has been so excellently done. And therefore the school of Rossetti has been thronged rather by the poetasters who desired to write rather than by the poets who have been constrained to sing.

In one important direction did he and his sister Christina and Mr. Swinburne, who may be held to have been the heads of the school, modify the literary art of the time. They effected a reformation in language. Poetry had fallen under the influence of Tennyson in an almost helpless fashion. Tennyson had himself lost his first virginal freshness, and in the idylls, and still more in the Enoch Arden volume, was tending to produce a certain empty form of blank verse, melodious indeed, and sweet as honey, but still conventional and tame. Poets like Lord Lytton and Coventry Patmore (though he later recovered, or rather won, a noble originality), had possessed themselves of the seed, and were able to grow the flower in luxuriant profusion. They could turn out glowing verse, but verse which was soft, mild, amiable, with a certain taint of thought which may be described as priggish and parochial.

Rossetti, Christina Rossetti, and Mr. Swinburne struck boldly across the path, leaving a trail of fire. They were not so much rebellious, but they did again what Tennyson had done in his early prime. They dared to use simple and direct words, which they infused with new and audacious charm; there was nothing didactic about them; they went straight to the source of pure beauty; they re-charged, so to speak, homely and direct expressions with the very element of poetical vigour.

Even Christina Rossetti, deeply religious as she is, had little ethical about her. She enjoyed her faith, if I may use the expression, with all the rapture of a mediæval saint; she visualised her dreams without timidity, and spoke her thoughts, not because they were improving, but because they were beautiful.

But in all this Rossetti was the leader; and this process of breaking up a dominant tradition, which requires to be done at frequent intervals, and which is done when art is really alive, reacted on Tennyson himself, and gave a new impulse to the stream of English poetry.

And so it may be said that his influence on poetry, like his influence on art, has been of a general rather than of a direct kind. He has stimulated the sense of beauty, the desire to extract the very essence of delight from emotion, and form, and colour; he has inculcated devotion to art, and profound intention, and deliberate isolation; but the upshot is that he stands alone, in a fever of sense and spirit, a figure clasping its hands in a poignancy of agitation, and rather overshadowed by the doom of art than crowned with its laurels.

CHAPTER VI

TRANSLATIONS—PROSE—LETTERS

ROSSETTI'S translations from the Early Italian Poets, together with the *Vita Nuova* of Dante, published in 1861, is a book of greater interest when considered in reference to the history of Rossetti's mind than as a literary performance. Popular it could never be. The whole frame of mind, the elaborate passion with its hot and cold fits, the feverish sensibility of the writers, the underlying thought that the passion of love is at once the guiding light and the business of life,—all this is very alien to the calmer English spirit, to which courtship is a time of inexplicable and gracious romance indeed, but takes its place in later life as a marvellous episode, enshrined in memory, the troubled entrance to a calm haven.

It is only too clear how congenial the atmosphere was to Rossetti, because the patient labour involved in the task is fairly marvellous to contemplate. The verse-translations occupy nearly four hundred pages of his collected works, and the *Vita Nuova* some sixty more. It is evident where Rossetti gained his rich vocabulary, his command of rhyme, his inexhaustible store of grave and dignified language. And, further, it is plain that the minute examination of archaic

Italian models exercised an extraordinary influence in the evolution of his own style.

An interesting preface, written in strong and nervous prose, is prefixed to the book in which Rossetti writes that "these poems possess, in their degree, beauties of a kind which can never again exist in art. . . . Nothing but a strong impression, first of their poetic value, and next of the biographical interest of some of them, . . . would have inclined me to bestow the time and trouble which have resulted in this collection."

In a very striking and valuable passage, Rossetti lays down firmly, and with real insight, the general principles of translation:—

"The life-blood of rhythmical translation is this commandment,—that a good poem shall not be turned into a bad one. The only true motive for putting poetry into a fresh language must be to endow a fresh nation, as far as possible, with one more possession of beauty. Poetry not being an exact science, literality of rendering is altogether secondary to this chief law. I say *literality*,—not fidelity, which is by no means the same thing. When literality can be combined with what is thus the primary condition of success, the translator is fortunate, and must strive his utmost to unite them; when such object can only be attained by paraphrase, that is his only path."

There follows a fine section which describes the difficulties and despairs of the translator; the obstacles of rhyme, the need to sacrifice his own taste in the matter of idiom, cadence, and structure:—

"Now he would slight the matter for the music, and now the music for the matter; but no,—he must deal to each alike. Sometimes too a flaw in the work galls him, and he would fain remove it, doing for the poet that which his age denied him; but no,—it is not in the bond. His path is like that of Aladdin through the enchanted vaults: many are the precious fruits and flowers which he must pass by unheeded in search for the lamp alone; happy if at last, when brought to light, it does not prove that his old lamp has been exchanged for a new one,—glittering indeed to the eye, but scarcely of the same virtue nor with the same genius at its summons."

The preface ends with a fine metaphor, conveying a rebuke under the form of a dignified apology:—
"I know that there is no great stir to be made by launching afresh, on high-seas busy with new traffic, the ships which have been long out-stripped and the ensigns which are grown strange."

The book also contains a carefully written Introduction, giving some biographical particulars about the authors of the poems. Rossetti writes first of the importance of the *Vita Nuova* to all who would fully comprehend the *Commedia*. "It is only from the perusal of its earliest and then undivulged self-communings that we can divine the whole bitterness of wrong to such a soul as Dante's, *its poignant sense of abandonment, or its deep and jealous refuge in memory.*" . . . "Throughout the *Vita Nuova* there is a strain like the first falling murmur which reaches the ear in some remote meadow, and prepares us to look upon the sea."

Once or twice in the introduction a certain fierceness breaks out against the over-interpretation of these poems. Speaking of a canzone of Guido Cavalcanti's, he writes:—

"A love-song which acts as such a fly-catcher for

priests and pedants looks very suspicious; and accordingly, on examination, it proves to be a poem beside the purpose of poetry, filled with metaphysical jargon, and perhaps the very worst of Guido's productions."

This impatience of pedantry, "*as beside the purpose of poetry*," manifests itself strongly at the end of the Introduction. "Among the severely edited books," he writes, "which had to be consulted in forming this collection, I have often suffered keenly from the buttonholders of learned Italy, who will not let one go on one's way; and have contracted a horror of those editions where the text, hampered with numerals for reference, struggles through a few lines at the top of the page only to stick fast at the bottom in a slough of verbal analysis. It would seem unpardonable to make a book which should be even as these."

He adds that he fears the Introduction will form "an awkward intermezzo" to the volume, but that it is necessary, "that so the reader may not find himself perpetually worried with footnotes during the consideration of something which may require a little peace. The glare of too many tapers is apt to render the altar-picture confused and inharmonious, even when their smoke does not obscure or deface it."

These extracts serve not only to show the purpose in Rossetti's mind in making the book, but illustrate very forcibly both the soundness and sanity of his criticism, and his strong, vigorous, and dignified prose. There is no preciosity of phrase; in homely and vigorous English he speaks out his thought, in lucid form and sternly compressed; while the little similes which light up the argument are like springs that break out beside a straight white road.

The qualities displayed by the translations are

directness and dignity. It was natural that Rossetti, of all poets the most self-willed, should move somewhat stiffly in the thoughts of others. Still his sympathy with both the associations and the mood of the poems was so vivid and intimate that it carried him safely through the ordeal.

Perhaps the poems where there is a wealth of brilliant images are those that most readily lend themselves to quotation. What could be more rich and delicate than the following sonnet from Guido Cavalcanti?—

"Beauty in woman; the high will's decree;
   Fair knighthood armed for manly exercise;
   The pleasant song of birds; love's soft replies;
The strength of rapid ships upon the sea;
The serene air when light begins to be;
   The white snow, without wind that falls and lies;
   Fields of all flower; the place where waters rise;
Silver and gold; azure in jewellery "—

all of which bright and solemn things he weighs against

"the sweet and quiet worth
Which my dear lady cherishes at heart,"

and finds them wanting.

Here again is a picture, from a ballad of Guido Cavalcanti's, with a picture just such as Rossetti might himself have conceived and painted—

"Within a copse I met a shepherd-maid,
  More fair, I said, than any star to see.

She came with waving tresses pale and bright,
  With rosy cheer, and loving eyes of flame,
Guiding the lambs beneath her wand aright.
  Her naked feet still had the dews on them,
    As, singing like a lover, so she came;
Joyful, and fashioned for all ecstasy."

Then in the didactic or philosophical sonnet we see the sober gravity in which he could move. In the sonnet by Enzo, King of Sardinia, on the *Fitness of Seasons*, after the octette which speaks of contrasted occasions,

> ". . . a time to talk, and hold thy peace ;
> A time to labour, and a time to cease,"

the conclusion of the matter runs—

> " Wherefore I hold him well-advised and sage
>   Who evermore keeps prudence facing him,
>   And lets his life slide with occasion ;
>   And so comports himself, through youth to age,
>   That never any man at any time
>   Can say, Not thus, but thus thou shouldst have done."

Or for perfect simplicity and loveliness consider the three stanzas from *The Young Girl*, a lyric by Niccolò Tommaséo, the brilliant Dalmatian poet, who died in 1874—

> " As in a gilded room
>   Shines 'mid the braveries
>   Some wild-flower, by the bloom
>   Of its delicate quietness
>   Recalling the forest-trees
>   In whose shadow it was,
>   And the water and the green grass :—
>
> .   .   .   .   .   .
>
>   Let the proud river-course,
>   That shakes its mane and champs,
>   Run between marble shores
>   By the light of many lamps,
>   While all the ooze and the damps
>   Of the city's choked-up ways
>   Make it their draining-place.

> Rather the little stream
> For me ; which, hardly heard,
> Unto the flower, its friend,
> Whispers as with a word.
> The timid journeying bird
> Of the pure drink that flows
> Takes but one drop, and goes."

The above poem may indeed be cited as an almost supreme instance of translation, where the outline, traced as it were above the gracious original, with absolute transparency of phrase, as Pater says, becomes a poem, which, like a quiet room seen in a mirror, gains a beauty and a mystery of its own.

The *Vita Nuova* in Rossetti's rendering has a dignified and archaic precision, but it is impossible to give any conception of its beauty by brief extracts. The style of the English Bible is generally followed, though the vocabulary is not strictly Biblical; but it will also be clear how easily the translator moves under the "excellent adjusted folds," and how complete a mastery he had over the vehicle of austere and lucid prose.

In point of fidelity to the spirit of his original, Rossetti's translations of the poems in the *Vita Nuova* probably surpass most other metrical renderings in our language, whether of Dante or any other poet. This was no more than was to have been expected, considering that his father's mystical bent had steeped his childhood in the Dantesque atmosphere, and that Italian was almost a mother tongue to him.

There are, however, more departures from the literal meaning of the original than would have been expected with Rossetti's genius and special advantages, and the very great pains he is known to have bestowed upon his work. These aberrations are almost always traceable to the endeavour to escape from difficulties, which is usually accomplished either by interpolating something not in the original, or by more or less deflecting Dante's meaning to bring in the rhyme desired by the translator.

Compared, nevertheless, with the liberties taken by other translators, Rossetti's licences seem venial; and if he sometimes introduces a thought or phrase not strictly warranted by his original, it is so fine as almost to appear an improvement upon it. I do not think he had any motive except to elude verbal difficulties; but the general tendency of his variations is, so to speak, to screw Dante's note up a little higher.

Yet after all, though Rossetti is hardly so exact as he might have been if he had kept verbal accuracy more strictly before him, or revised his work with a special view to this object, when he is literal, he is literal with a delicacy and vividness that no other translator approaches, and makes one almost feel that Dante's own expression would have followed the same bias, if Dante had been writing in English.

In reading Rossetti's original prose writings, one is tempted to regret that he did not write more prose. He had a strong sense of balance and proportion, a vivid descriptive gift, and a very rich vocabulary. There was a certain largeness and prodigality of thought and language within him, which was thwarted and confined by the selective process of poetry, and which might have been nobly and freely employed outside the fashioning of those small jewelled sonnets. But prose was alien to his disposition. His mind and temperament demanded something more distinctive, deliberate, remote, formal—the precise embodiment of dreams.

He wrote as he painted, in a sort of solemn stateliness, building up, touch by touch, a picture or a poem. Magnificence and gorgeousness of texture were of the very essence of his art, and the writing of prose doubtless seemed to him a homely and uninspiring business, hardly worthy of one whose conception of beauty was very high. Both in his talk and in his familiar letters there was an entire absence of anything affected or pompous. His natural mode of expression was brisk, incisive, penetrating; but artistic presentment was for him a thing apart, a pontifical and ceremonious matter, and he drew a very sharp line between what was appropriate to ordinary intercourse,—where he said and wrote just what was in his mind, with the impressiveness of an able, critical, and somewhat intolerant character,—and what was appropriate to the deliberate service of art. If Rossetti had set himself to write prose, it is obvious from what remains that he might have taken a high rank among prose writers. But besides the two early compositions *Hand and Soul*, and *St. Agnes of Intercession*, which is unfinished, there is nothing of an original kind, apart from his correspondence. The matter that he contributed to Gilchrist's *Life of Blake* is the most important prose work of his later years; and there is a certain amount of art criticism, and a little literary criticism which has only a secondary value. In these latter writings, his eager generosity, his determination to see and recognise whatever was good, is almost too liberally emphasised at the expense of his critical judgment.

Hand and Soul is a romance with a careful circumstantial setting. It is an imaginary episode in the life of a young painter called Chiaro dell'Erma, a native of Arezzo, who hears of the famous painter, Giunta Pisano, and determines to become his pupil. On arriving at Pisa and entering the studio, he soon becomes aware that he knows more of art than the master can teach him, and is drawn aside into the vivid enjoyment of social life. From this purposeless existence he is aroused by hearing mentioned the name of a young painter, Bonaventura, who, it is said, bids fair to be a rival of Giunta. Chiaro awakes like a man out of a pleasant dream, and throws himself wholly into the pursuit of art. Three years of work bring him fame, but he is not satisfied; there falls upon him a deeper hunger of the spirit: he recognises that his ideals have been of the earth, that he has been content with the mere worship of beauty and the recognition of the world. He determines to devote his art to "the presentment of some moral greatness that should influence the beholder." But in carrying this out, he finds that he has lost his power over the hearts and imaginations of men; and he recognises that he is no nearer the enjoyment of that interior peace which alone is worth striving for. One day there is a great festival at Pisa; Chiaro has no heart to join the simple-minded throng, but sits in his balcony looking out upon the porch of San Petronio, and the crowd that goes and comes. In the porch are some frescoes which he himself has painted, representing Peace in an allegory, and he sees with horror and dismay a fight take place in the street between two rival factions, in which swords are drawn and his frescoes bespattered with blood.

Then he sees that he has failed in his highest ideal

as well, and that he has no direct influence upon the world such as he desires.

Then he is suddenly aware of the presence in his room of a lady of marvellous beauty, austere but gentle, who speaks to him and tells him that she is the image of his own very soul. She tells him that though he has failed both in his pursuit of fame and in the higher pursuit of faith, yet because he has not followed meaner ends, such as wealth or ease, there is hope yet. Then she tells him that he must make a wise and humble sacrifice; that God is strong and has no *need* of him, that he has erred in thinking that he can help God. He must set himself humbly to serve, and to paint his own innermost spirit.

Then she bids him paint her as she stands; and afterwards he falls asleep. There the story ceases; and to this is appended a circumstantial account by the author of his finding in the Pitti Gallery—the number and the room are given—a wonderful portrait of a woman, with the words "*Manus animam pinxit*" and a date; the author listens to a contemptuous dialogue of Italian and French art-students about the picture—and so the narrative ends.

It may be added that the circumstantial nature of the details mystified many readers. There are instances on record of people looking for the picture, and expressing to Rossetti disappointment that it was no longer there. Rossetti seems to have enjoyed the little mystery, though always frankly avowing that the tale was a pure invention.

Beside the autobiographical interest, the actual writing is of a singularly pure and lofty type. It is wonderful to reflect that the greater part of it was written in a single night; but this gives it a unity and spontaneity that increase the charm. The sentences move with a certain stiffness, and the language is for the most part archaic in colour, of an antique precision and grace, strongly reminiscent of the Book of Job, though there is a certain mingling of modern terms. The whole has an exquisite formal simplicity of expression that gives it an indefinable flavour of beauty. A few passages may be quoted from it. The effect of beauty upon the sensitive apprehension of Chiaro is indicated in a sentence which recalls Leonardo da Vinci—"he would feel faint in sunsets and at the sight of stately persons,"—and the description of Chiaro himself is naively told :—

"Women loved Chiaro; for, in despite of the burthen of study, he was well-favoured and very manly in his walking; and, seeing his face in front, there was a glory upon it, as upon the face of one who feels a light round his hair."

Again, there are many passages of an obscure beauty, where an image is hinted rather than told in detail. At the first sight of the mystical lady of his soul :—

"He was like one who, scaling a great steepness, hears his own voice echoed in some place much higher than he can see, *and the name of which is not known to him.*"

There are many flashes of deep insight throughout the tale. Thus of the emulous passion which rises in the aspiring soul, he writes :—

"Or, at times, when he could not paint, he would sit for hours in thought of all the greatness the world had known from of old; until he was weak with yearning, like one who gazes upon a path of stars."

But where the Soul speaks to him, the whole narrative rises into a higher and more prophetic strain. The following is a noble passage, declaring the truth that the artist must be content to have given joy to others, even though he lacks the fruition of fame :—

"For Fame, in noble soils, is a fruit of the Spring: but not therefore should it be said: 'Lo! my garden that I planted is barren: the crocus is here, but the lily is dead in the dry ground, and shall not lift the earth that covers it: therefore I will fling my garden together, and give it unto the builders.' Take heed rather that thou trouble not the *wise secret earth*; for in the mould that thou throwest up shall the first tender growth lie to waste; which else had been made strong in its season. Yea, and even if the year fall past in all its months, and the soil be indeed, to thee, peevish and incapable, and though thou indeed gather all thy harvest, and it suffice for others, and thou remain vexed with emptiness; and others drink of thy streams, and the drouth rasp thy throat;—let it be enough that these have found the feast good, and thanked the giver: remembering that, when the winter is striven through, there is another year, whose wind is meek, and whose sun fulfilleth all."

In these latter passages the influence of the prophetic books of the Old Testament is unmistakable; the sentences have the detached cadences of Hebrew poetry. But what is more interesting than the manner, is the intensity of spiritual vision which the whole reveals. It is a confession of Faith of the most intimate kind. I believe that there exists no document more vital to the understanding of the principles on which Rossetti worked, and the lofty conception of art thus formulated. Few of Rossetti's fellow-labourers could have sketched so noble an ideal; and we may be grateful that one whose hatred of any assumption of superiority, any pompous enunciation of lofty aims, was so sincere, did for once draw aside the veil from a secluded spirit, and reveal his deepest and most sacred dreams. Whether this source of inspiration abode with Rossetti through his life, or whether it was a vision of truth seen in a moment of generous insight, and to which he failed to be true, is hard to judge. Certainly in later days he kept silence on these matters, or else his thoughts are not recorded. He certainly never pursued wealth or fame for its own sake; it may perhaps be thought that, like Solomon, he was drawn aside from the austerer vision by the seductions of sense, and, as Keat's knight, fell under the spell of *La Belle Dame Sans Merci*. Perhaps, like the pilgrim of the legend, he strayed in among the dusky groves of the Hill of Venus, and bowed his knee to other gods. We dare not say. He never deliberately abandoned the faith of his youth, and he always strove to let the hand paint the soul. But it is difficult not to feel that a spirit nurtured on such thoughts as these, that thus greeted him upon the threshold of days, might have reached a wider and richer development both in art and life.

The story called *St. Agnes of Intercession* was originally to have been called *An Autopsychology*, and was intended for the *Germ*. It was begun in 1848 or 1849, and was never finished. Rossetti was planning to finish it in his last illness, but apparently did not even begin to do so. It is a strange, mystical story, and is mainly interesting from the autobiographical passages which occur in it, and which have already been quoted. The story is told by an art-student who, as a child, finds a picture of St. Agnes in glory, by an old master, Bucciuolo Angiolieri. He is curiously attracted by this. When he reaches man's estate he meets a beautiful girl, Miss Mary Arden, and becomes engaged to her. Miss Arden sits to him for the central figure of a large picture which he is painting. It is exhibited, and being hung on the line attracts great attention. The painter goes to the exhibition and meets an art critic there, who is described so minutely, that it seems probable that some personal satire is intended. The critic sees the picture, and commenting upon it, says that the central figure reminds him of the work of Angiolieri. The painter becomes suddenly aware of an extraordinary likeness between Miss Arden and the St. Agnes. He determines to see the picture itself, and goes to Italy, where, after searching in vain in several galleries for it, he finds it at Perugia, and learns that the picture was painted by Angiolieri from his affianced mistress, who sat to him when in the grip of mortal illness, and actually died while the picture was being painted. He then goes to Lucca, and finds a picture of Angiolieri, painted by the artist's own hand, in which he recognises, with a shock of terror, his own features. He hurries home, with a fever upon him, and on his return has a long illness. Here the narrative breaks off. But the intended conclusion is known from an etching which Millais prepared to illustrate the story, and which still exists, from which it is clear that Miss Arden was to have sat to him for another picture, and was to have died while being painted. Moreover, a little water-colour of Rossetti's, called *Bonifazio's Mistress*, representing a girl dying while sitting for her portrait to her lover, is in reality a design for the same scene.

The story is diffusely told, and is written in modern English with no flavour of archaism. It has no great literary interest, from the point of view of style; but it illustrates the mystical supernaturalism which lay very deep in Rossetti's character.

The only other piece of deliberate prose writing, except a few reviews and criticisms of pictures, is the contribution Rossetti made to Gilchrist's *Life of Blake*.

Rossetti in 1847 had purchased for ten shillings a MS. book of Blake's, containing a quantity of fragments of prose and verse, and some designs. It is interesting to note that there were in this book a number of gibes and jeers against certain accepted painters, such as Correggio, Titian, Rubens, Rembrandt, Reynolds, and Gainsborough, whom Blake thought exuberant, or liable to disguise tenuity of thought by tricks of manner. The volume was borrowed from Rossetti by Alexander Gilchrist, who was then preparing Blake's *Life*, which was published in 1863. Gilchrist died prematurely before the book was finished, and Rossetti, with characteristic generosity, helped Mrs. Gilchrist with the critical part of the biography, wrote a considerable passage, and edited some of the poems included.

He wrote, while he was doing the work, that he found it necessary to go to the British Museum to study the coloured works of Blake, adding, "All I could think of was to dwell on some of these. Facts, and descriptions of facts, are in my line; but to talk *about* a thing merely is what I could never well manage." He says again that it is useless to attempt to comment on individual poems. "The truth is that, as regards such a poem as *My Spectre*, I do not understand it a bit better than anybody else; only I know, better than some may know, that it has claims as poetry apart from the question of understanding it, and is therefore worth printing."

The whole passage is vigorous, and the criticism is sound and judicious. It contains not only some striking enunciations of artistic principles, but some beautiful pieces of descriptive writing.

"Tenderness," he writes, "the constant unison of wonder and familiarity so mysteriously allied in nature, the sense of fulness and abundance such as we feel in a field, not because we pry into it all, but because it is all there: these are the inestimable prizes to be secured only by such study in the painter's every picture."

He describes with great felicity Blake's "prismatic" system of colour—and the "spiritual quality [of his designs] which always mingles with their truth to nature," the combination of "subtle and exquisite reality" and "ideal grandeur"; "whether we find him dealing with the pastoral sweetness of drinking cattle at a stream, their hides and fleeces all glorified by sunset with magic rainbow hues; or revealing to us, in a flash of creative genius, *some parted sky and beaten sea full of portentous expectation.*"

Again, nothing could be more masterly, more penetrative, than the following descriptions of Blake's designs:—"such conceptions as painter never before dreamed of: some old skeleton folded together in the dark bowels of earth or rock, discoloured with metallic stain and vegetable mould; some symbolic human

birth of crowned flowers at dawn, amid rosy light
and the joyful opening of all things."

Or again, in the description of the designs for the
Book of Job:—"Here, at the base, are sheepfolds
watched by shepherds; up the sides is a trellis, on
whose lower rings birds sit upon their nests, while
angels, on the higher ones, worship round flame and
cloud, till it arches at the summit into a sky full of
the written words of God."

The criticisms on Blake's poems display a delicate
sympathy and a power of entering into the original
conception. Yet they are always balanced; he warns
the student of Blake against "seeking for a sense more
recondite than was really meant." But as a spiritual
commentary on Blake's work these criticisms have a
profoundly stimulating effect, especially in a beautiful
passage too long to quote here, commenting very fully
on the poem *Broken Love*.

To illustrate another side of Rossetti's power of
expression, his reply to *The Fleshly School of Poetry*
is most dignified in manner, and moreover affords
a good instance of his command over simple, nervous,
unaffected English. It appeared in the *Athenæum* for
December 16, 1871. Rossetti rebuts Buchanan's
criticism on the lines which he had quoted from the
first of the four sonnets entitled *Willowwood*:—

" And as I stooped, her own lips rising there
    Bubbled with brimming kisses at my mouth."

He continues:—"The critic has quoted (as I said)
only the last two lines, and he has italicised the
second as something unbearable and ridiculous. Of
course the inference would be that this was really

my own absurd bubble-and-squeak notion of an actual kiss. The reader will perceive at once, from the whole sonnet transcribed above, how untrue such an inference would be. The sonnet describes a dream or trance of divided love momentarily re-united by the longing fancy; and in the imagery of the dream, the face of the beloved rises through deep dark waters to kiss the lover. Thus the phrase, 'Bubbled with brimming kisses,' etc., bears purely on the special symbolism employed, and from that point of view will be found, I believe, perfectly simple and just."

The above passage shows that the urgency of the controversy did not deprive Rossetti of his sense of humour.

Indeed, the whole defence is wonderfully restrained and temperate, though it glows with a fierce heat of inner indignation, and is in strong contrast with the view that afterwards unhappily took possession of Rossetti's mind, exasperated by morbid brooding and weakened by an enervating anodyne.

Rossetti may fairly be ranked among the best writers of familiar letters. A large number have been published, and the "Family Letters" in vol. ii. of Mr. W. M. Rossetti's *Letters and Memoirs*, the letters to William Allingham, edited by Dr. Birkbeck Hill, and the extracts given by Mr. Hall Caine in the *Recollections*, contain the most important.

Rossetti wrote as he talked, entirely without affectation, and as a rule in a vein of robust cheerfulness. At the same time there are in the "Family Letters," in which he appears in his most lovable light, many passages of the most loyal and tender affection.

He did not indulge much in description, saying on one occasion, "Landscape-letters are things to me impossible," but when he did so, he touched the characteristics of a scene with wonderful felicity.

It would be difficult to publish a just selection of the letters, because in the first place they are very allusive, and require a good deal of explanatory comment, and in the second place they are so interwoven with small personal detail as to render selection very difficult.

Rossetti, when younger, liked writing, "even business letters," as he once said. In early days at Cheyne Walk he designed an elaborate device for his letter-paper,[1] and had it printed on fine handmade paper; but with characteristic indolence about small matters, when the original stock was exhausted, it was seldom or never replenished, and many of the letters are written on any paper he could get hold of at a moment's notice. In later life he found writing more tiresome, and there are many allusions in his letters to his own dilatoriness as a correspondent. His handwriting was at first small, and almost niggling, but he acquired, as years went on, a fine, masterful, clear hand, very bold in sweep and outline, which only at the end grew tremulous and uncertain. The greater part of the family letters take their origin in some matter of small business or domestic arrangement, but those which he wrote to Allingham have much more deliberate criticism of a light kind; he wrote freely of the books he was reading, and of the people among whom he was living.

[1] A double circle, containing on the right his monogram, and on the left a flourishing tree, with the motto FRANGAS NON FLECTAS, copied from a seal of his father's.

The letters to Mr. Caine, though they contain some of the most valuable of his critical dicta, were written under more melancholy auspices, when he was living a secluded life and besieged by hypochondriacal fancies. Yet the relation in which he found himself to Mr. Caine —that of the veteran man of letters confronted with the enthusiasm of a young and critically sympathetic admirer—called out a generous affection on Rossetti's part, which proves how grateful he was for appreciation, and how ready to place the resources of his mind at the disposal of one who understood him. But still there is a shadow and a weariness over this correspondence, absent from the Allingham letters, which bubble out like a spring into the sunshine.

Nothing comes out more clearly than his sympathetic observation of animals, and the chronicles of Dizzy, the Kelmscott dog, are worthy to be ranked with Cowper's letters about his hares.

I subjoin a few extracts which may illustrate some of the special characteristics of the letters. But it must be said that they pre-eminently deserve to be read in their entirety, and that the setting of current affairs and personal topics in which the more deliberate passages are framed are not the least part of their charm :—

To William Allingham (1854).

"I like Mac Crac pretty well enough.... My stern treatment of him was untempered by even a moment's weakness. I told him I had nothing whatever to show him, and that his picture was not begun, which placed us at once on a perfect understanding. He seems hard up."

To William Allingham.

November 1854.

"Have you seen anything of W. B. Scott's volume? I may be able to send it you sooner or later, if you like. The title-page has a vignette with the words 'Poems by a Painter' printed very gothically indeed. A copy being sent to old Carlyle, he did not read any of the poems, but read the title, 'Poems by a Printer.' He wrote off at once to the imaginary printer to tell him to stick to his types and give up his metaphors. Woolner saw the book lying at Carlyle's, heard the story, and told him of his mistake, at which he had the decency to seem a little annoyed, as he knows Scott, and esteems him and his family. Now that we are allied with Turkey, we might think seriously of the bastinado for that old man, on such occasions as the above."

To William Allingham, speaking of possible improvements in one of his own engravings (1855).

"I showed the proof yesterday to Woolner, who saw the original drawing, and he was as shocked as myself. Nevertheless . . . it would be possible to improve it a good deal, I believe—not by adding shadows . . . but by cutting out lines, by which means the human character might be partially substituted for the oyster and goldfish cast of features, and other desirable changes effected."

To William Allingham.

14 CHATHAM PLACE, BLACKFRIARS.
(End of 1856.)

". . . To-day here is neither a bright day nor a dark day, but a white smutty day,—piebald,—wherein, accordingly, life seems neither worth keeping nor getting rid of. The thick sky has a thin red sun stuck in the middle of it, like the specimen wafer stuck outside a box of them. Even if you turned back the lid, there would be nothing behind it, be sure, but a jumble of such flat dead suns. I am going to sleep."

To William Allingham.

(*Postmark—December* 18, 1856.)

"The piece of news freshest in my mind is *Aurora Leigh*,— an astounding work, surely. You said nothing of it. I know that St. Francis and Poverty do not wed in these days, in St. James' Church, with rows of portrait figures on either side, and the corners neatly finished with angels. I know that if a blind man were to enter the room this evening and talk to me for some hours, I should, with the best intentions, be in danger of twigging his blindness before the right moment came, if such there were, for the chord in the orchestra and the proper theatrical start ; yet with all my knowledge I have felt something like a bug ever since reading *Aurora Leigh*. Oh, the wonder of it ! and oh, the bore of writing about it.

"The Brownings are long gone back now, and with them one of my delights,— an evening resort where I never felt unhappy. How large a part of the real world, I wonder, are those two small people ?—taking meanwhile so little room in any railway carriage, and hardly needing a double bed at the inn."

To Ford Madox Brown.

CHEYNE WALK, 1866.

". . . I was very sorry to bolt in that way so early from such a really jolly party as yours. But, Brown, if you had known ! Doubtless you, in common with your guests, admired my elegant languor and easy grace. But O Brown, had Truth herself been there to rend away my sheltering coat ! Behold me ! [Picture of D. G. R. with bursting coat, etc., called *Physical condition and mental attitude.*]

"The burden of conscious fat and hypocrisy, the stings of remorse, the haunting dread of exposure as every motion wafted the outer garment to this side or to that, the senses quickened to catch the fatal sound of further rents—all this and more—but let us draw once more over the scene that veil which Fate respected. Might not Tupper say truly, 'Let not Man, fattening, leave his dress-trowsers too long unworn, lest a worse thing come unto him ' ?—Your affectionate D. G. R."

To his Mother from Kelmscott (1873).

". . . On Thursday George was at a wedding at Manchester, and during his absence Dizzy returned for a while to his cuneiform stage of aspect and demeanour. He has been very funny in various ways. On one occasion we got a musical instrument —a dulcimer, which lies flat on the ground—and put a bit of sugar on the strings. Then, as Dizzy approached to take it, the strings were immediately struck with the plectrum, and the contest of terror and appetite in Dizzy's bosom was delicious. On one occasion an attempt was made, in his interest, to reduce him to a diet of dog-biscuit. He became gradually more and more dejected, until one morning he ate a stone instead, which, reappearing on the hearthrug, convinced his master that he must not be reduced to despair again. Whenever he wants to be petted, his plan is to eat a bit of crab-apple, or something he obviously would not eat if he could help it. An outcry of compassion is the immediate result, followed by successive courses of kidneys, macaroni, etc."

To Mr. Hall Caine (1880).

"It is an awful fact that sun, moon, or candlelight once looked down on the human portent of Dr. Johnson and Mrs. Hannah More convened in solemn conclave above the outspread sonnets of Milton, with a meritorious and considerate resolve of finding out for him 'why they were so bad.' This is so stupendous a warning, that perhaps it may even incline one to find some of them better than they are."

To Mr. Hall Caine (who was then making an anthology of sonnets) (1880).

"'How are they [the poets] to be approached?'—you innocently ask. Ye heavens! how does the cat's-meat-man approach Grimalkin?—and what is that relation in life when compared to the *rapport* established between the living bard and the fellow-creature who is disposed to cater to his caterwauling appetite for publicity?"

But it is very nearly impossible to give any idea of the charm of such letters by quoting a few extracts; and the above passages are as inadequate to illustrate the free and vigorous beauty of the original, as entomological specimens pinned in a collector's cabinet to suggest the bright insects that upon a rosebed in midsummer open and shut their rainbow wings.

I will here add a few scattered critical dicta of Rossetti's, from letters and recorded talk. What, for instance, could be more vigorous than the following maxim which occurs in a letter of 1873 to Mr. Gosse?—

"It seems to me that all poetry, to be really enduring, is bound to be as *amusing* (however trivial the word may sound) as any other class of literature; and I do not think that enough amusement to keep it alive can ever be got out of incidents not amounting to events."

This is a truth which is not only often neglected, but is sacrificed to a false ideal of literary dignity. I suppose that Rossetti used the word in the sense of interesting, and not in the conversational sense of laughable. It is, perhaps, a reminiscence of the use of the word by Dr. Johnson, who calls *Coriolanus* "one of the most amusing" of Shakespeare's plays in the sense of "abounding in dramatic interest."

Again:—"Poetry should seem to the hearer to have been always present to his thought, but never before heard."

Again:—"Moderation is the highest law of poetry. Experimental as Coleridge sometimes becomes, his *best* work is tuned but never twanged; and this is his great distinction from almost all others who venture as far." Again, embodying one of the most memorable literary dicta ever enunciated, he wrote to Mr. Hall Caine:—

"You have much too great a habit of speaking of a special octave, sestette, or line. Conception, my boy, FUNDAMENTAL BRAINWORK, that is what makes the difference in all art. Work your metal as much as you like, but first take care that it is gold and worth working. A Shakspearean sonnet is better than the most perfect in form, because Shakspeare wrote it."

Again, what could be a more felicitous description of a certain class of lyric than the following? Rossetti is speaking of Sydney Dobell's poem *Keith of Ravelston*, which he greatly admired:—

"I have always regarded that poem as being one of the finest, of its length, in any modern poet; ranking with Keats's *La Belle Dame Sans Merci*, and the other masterpieces of the condensed and hinted order so dear to imaginative minds."

The above criticisms all seem to me to show the hard intellectual force, so distinct from the dreamy character with which Rossetti is generally credited, which he brought to bear on his art. There is no vagueness or looseness about them; he goes straight down to fundamental principles. Nothing proves more conclusively the sanity and sense of Rossetti's critical power than his discussion of particular authors. He had very strong preferences, but he never, so to speak, swallowed an author whole, except, perhaps, in the case of Chatterton, nor was in the least blinded either by prestige or by his own admiration.

Many admirable fragments of literary criticism occur in various letters, though of course it must be borne in mind that they are informal criticisms, written off on the spur of the moment, and not deliberately formed and expressed. It will be clear, I think, that he had a strong perceptive judgment; but that his synthetic power of criticism was weak as compared to his analytic insight; that he could estimate the value of a particular poem or a particular author, but that he had little taste for critical comparison.

The following, to Mr. Caine, contains an admirable forecast of the probable development in the case of Keats and Shelley, both of whom he ranked very high:—

"I am truly delighted to hear how young you are. In original work, a man does some of his best things by your time of life, though he only finds it out in a rage much later, at some date when he expected to know no longer that he had ever done them. Keats hardly died so much too early—not at all if there had been any danger of his taking to the modern habit eventually—treating material as product, and shooting it all out as it comes. Of course, however, he wouldn't; he was getting always choicer and simpler, and my favourite piece in his works is *La Belle Dame Sans Merci*—I suppose about his last. As to Shelley, it is really a mercy that he has not been hatching yearly universes till now. He might, I suppose; for his friend Trelawny still walks the earth without great-coat, stockings, or underclothing, this Christmas [1879]. In criticism, matters are different, as to seasons of production. . . . I am writing hurriedly and horribly in every sense. Write on the subject again, and I'll try to answer better. All greetings to you."

Again of Keats and Shelley he wrote:—

"You quote some of Keats's sayings. One of the

most characteristic I think is in a letter to Haydon:—
'I value more the privilege of seeing great things in loneliness, than the fame of a prophet.' I had not in mind the quotations you give from Keats as bearing on the poetic (or prophetic) mission of 'doing good.' I must say that I should not have thought a longer career thrown away upon him (as you intimate) if he had continued to the age of anything only to give joy. Nor would he ever have done any 'good' at all. Shelley did good, and perhaps some harm with it. Keats's joy was after all a flawless gift.

"Keats wrote to Shelley:—'You, I am sure, will forgive me for sincerely remarking that you might curb your magnanimity and be more of an artist, and load every rift of your subject with ore.' Cheeky!—but not so much amiss. Poetry, and no prophecy, however, must come of that mood,—and no pulpit would have held Keats's wings,—the body and mind together were not heavy enough for a counterweight."

Coleridge, again, was an author whom Rossetti admired very deeply: "I worship him on the right side of idolatry," he wrote; and it adds a pathetic interest to the fact to realise that he saw in the tragic and blighted career of Coleridge a sad likeness to his own sufferings. Thus he wrote to Mr. Caine:—

"About Coleridge (whom I only view as a poet, his other aspects being to my apprehension mere bogies) I conceive the leading point about his work is its human love, and the leading point about his career, the sad fact of how little of it was devoted to that work. These are the points made in my sonnet, and the last is such as I (alas!) can sympathise with, though what has excluded more poetry with me (*mountains* of it

I don't want to heap) has chiefly been livelihood necessity."

The following are a few of Rossetti's impromptu judgments on various writers; they show both his intolerance and his insight. Of Longfellow and Walt Whitman he wrote to Allingham in 1856:—

"How I loathe *Wishi-washi*,[1]—of course without reading it. I have not been so happy in loathing anything for a long while—except, I think, *Leaves of Grass*, by that Orson of yours. I should like just to have the writing of a valentine to him in one of the reviews."

It is clear, however, at this date, that Rossetti had not read *Leaves of Grass*. He only spoke from hearsay, and from having seen a few lines and passages quoted in reviews. Still, he never wholly altered his mind about Whitman, because he felt that in his neglect of form and due proportion he was sacrificing what was, after all, what Allingham called " the most inalienable quality of a poem."

Again, he makes an interesting comparison of Oliver Madox Brown and Chatterton, the latter of whom he regarded with a singular admiration:—

"Oliver was the product of the most teeming hot-beds of art and literature, and even of compulsory addiction to the art of painting, in which nevertheless he was rapidly becoming as much a proficient as in literature. What he would have been if, like the ardent and heroic Chatterton, he had had to fight a single-handed battle for art and bread together against merciless mediocrity in high places,—what he would

[1] Longfellow's *Hiawatha*.

then have become, I cannot in the least calculate; but we know what Chatterton became."

The following is an admirable criticism:—

"I've been greatly interested in *Wuthering Heights*, the first novel I've read for an age, and the best (as regards power and sound style) for two ages, except *Sidonia*.[1] But it is a fiend of a book,—an incredible monster, combining all the stronger female tendencies from Mrs. Browning to Mrs. Brownrigg.[2] The action is laid in hell,—only it seems places and people have English names there."

At an early date his chief enthusiasm was for Browning. And in this connection it is interesting to note what he says after a visit he had just paid to Browning's home:—

"The father and uncle [of Browning]—father especially—show just that submissive yet highly cheerful and capable simplicity of character which often, I think, appears in the family of a great man who uses at last what the others have kept for him."

It is remarkable that he never did Wordsworth justice; but the ideals of the two were so radically dissimilar, that it is not surprising. Rossetti above all things disliked being, as it were, preached to from a superior platform; and this attribute in Wordsworth perhaps blinded him to the magnificence of much of his work. He resented Wordsworth's sacerdotal attitude, combined with a touch of the showman, towards Nature. To Allingham he wrote of Wordsworth, "He's good, you know, but unbearable."

[1] *Sidonia the Sorceress*, by Wilhelm Meinhold (author of *The Amber Witch*).
[2] The 'Prenti-cide, executed at Newgate.

Again, speaking more in detail of Wordsworth, Rossetti wrote:—

"With the verdicts given throughout . . . I generally sympathise, but not with the unqualified homage to Wordsworth. A reticence almost invariably present is fatal in my eyes to the highest pretensions on behalf of his sonnets. Reticence is but a poor sort of muse, nor is tentativeness (so often to be traced in his work) a good accompaniment in music. Take the sonnet on *Toussaint L'Ouverture* (in my opinion his noblest, and very noble indeed) and study (from Main's [1] note) the lame and fumbling changes made in various editions of the early lines, which remain lame in the end. Far worse than this, study the relation of the closing lines of his famous sonnet *The World is too much with us*, etc., to a passage in Spenser, and say whether plagiarism was ever more impudent or manifest (again I derive from Main's excellent exposition of the point), and then consider whether a bard was likely to do this once and yet not to do it often. Primary vital impulse was surely not fully developed in his muse."

The above are only instances taken at random of Rossetti's literary judgments, and many more will be found scattered up and down his correspondence. But they constitute, I think, a very remarkable body of critical dicta, worthy of the maturity of the man who at the age of thirteen or fourteen could detect that an Italian lyric, *A Clori*, in a privately printed volume by his grandfather, Gaetano Polidori, was an adaptation of Sir Henry Wotton's "You meaner beauties of the night."

[1] Main's *Treasury of English Sonnets*. Blackwood, 1880.

CHAPTER VII

PAINTING

It is loosely said that Rossetti is the most pictorial of poets, and the most literary of painters. Such a statement has a certain superficial truth about it. He lived strongly in both worlds; he drew designs for his poems, and he wrote sonnets for his pictures. But his most characteristic work, the *House of Life*, is in no sense pictorial poetry: he is not, for instance, so pictorial a poet as Keats, Tennyson, or William Morris. If Tennyson had been a painter, it would have been easy to point to the galleries of word-landscapes with which he adorned his poems. Again, with Rossetti, the most characteristic of his pictures, the kind which by the superficially informed person he is supposed always to have painted—the half-length designs of mystical women, mainly of three very notable types—these have no special literary quality.

The scope of this little volume, which is to present Rossetti as a man of letters, does not permit the question of his pictorial art to be treated exhaustively. But it may be remembered that Ruskin deliberately said of him, "I believe that Rossetti's name should be placed first on the list of men, within my own range of knowledge, who have raised and changed the spirit of modern art; raised it in absolute attainment, changed in direction of temper." So close a parallel exists between Rossetti's pictorial and his poetical work, that it is necessary to indicate the lines on which he worked.

In both poems and pictures there is the same ardent imagination, the same firm, intellectual conception, the same patient and elaborate method traceable.

The artistic influences under which Rossetti first fell cannot be very definitely indicated. He never went to Italy, but he studied Italian pictures carefully in the National Gallery and the Dulwich Gallery, and such private collections as those at Stafford House and Bridgewater House. He cared little for engravings or reproductions of pictures, though in later life he collected photographs of works which he admired. In his early visit to Paris he expresses certain preferences in art, as for Flandrin and Ingres. In 1849, however, when he visited Bruges, he fell for a time under the fascination of Memling and Van Eyck, and it is interesting to note that he considered the former to be the greater man, on the ground of his intellectual superiority.

But it cannot be said that Flemish art left any very marked effect on Rossetti's work. He was really only deeply affected by Italian painting, and especially in the direction of colour by the Venetian School.

The great artistic influence which was brought to bear on him in England was through the work of Ford Madox Brown. Madox Brown was a man of very high original genius, whose power was never really recognised in England until after his death. He was not a conciliatory person, and he embarked early in a quarrel with the Academy which had disastrous effects upon his fame. Ford Madox Brown differed from other English artists of the period in the fact that he had been strongly influenced by the French School, whereas other artists went to Italy for their inspiration. Madox Brown worked at Bruges, Ghent, Antwerp (under Baron Wappers), Paris, and finally Rome. He said of himself, however, that his art was not Belgian nor Parisian, but Spanish. And he characteristically wrote, "In Paris I first formed my idea of making my pictures real, because no French artist at the time did so."

English art was at a low ebb in all departments. The great school of portrait-painters, Reynolds, Romney, Raeburn, and Lawrence, had expired. The "grand" style flared up and out with such artists as Benjamin West, Fuseli, and Haydon. The great school of poetical landscape-painters, fathered by Gainsborough and Morland, was represented by such painters as Callcott, Thomas Creswick, Stanfield, and Frederick Lee, all good executants, but vitiated by a certain artificiality of methods. The meteoric force of Turner, with his transcendental treatment of Nature, was a thing by itself, and can hardly be said to have influenced the Pre-Raphaelites at all; though there is among the Rossetti papers one interesting statement of Mr. Holman Hunt's, made in early days, where he places Turner first among landscape-painters; and a still more interesting statement of Mr. Whistler's of the same date condemning Turner on the ground that he does not meet either the simply natural or the decorative requirements of landscape art, which to him appeared the only alternatives.

Otherwise the *genre* school of English painting had

fallen under the frankest *bourgeois* influence, as in the case of a painter of true genius such as Landseer. There was an entire absence of loftiness of motive and poetical intention. It is hardly an exaggeration to say that in the Royal Academy, in the early part of the century, the teaching was Italian, the colouring German, the painting Flemish, and the inspiration plain unadorned British, generally commonplace, and indeed namby-pamby.

Two painters may be held to have anticipated the Pre-Raphaelite method, Dyce and Noël Paton; but the former, though an artist of high genius, was a much occupied man, and only painted fitfully, while the latter was lacking in the highest inspiration. Dyce was among the first to realise the merits of the Pre-Raphaelite painters. Ruskin, in a letter to M. Chesneau (28th Dec. 1882), says that it was Dyce "who dragged me literally up to the picture of the *Carpenter's Shop*,[1] which I had passed disdainfully, and forced me to look for its merits."

But Madox Brown, possessing a great fertility of poetical invention and a marvellous intellectual grasp of subject, and deliberately eschewing all melodramatic or theatrical devices (though he did not always escape them), was exactly the kind of mind to appeal to Rossetti.

The Pre-Raphaelite theories have already been described, but it may be added that the stiffness and precision of the early works was an attempt not to copy the Italian painters, but to produce an effect of *naiveté* and sincerity; with the result that many of the uninitiated viewed them in the same light as Maro-

[1] *Christ in the House of His Parents* is the usual title.

chetti, when Ruskin brought out for his inspection "the violently variegated segments and angular anatomies of Lancelot and Guenevere at the grave of King Arthur"—and thereby produced, as Ruskin says, on the "bronze-minded sculptor simply the effect of a Knave of Clubs and Queen of Diamonds." It is remarkable to note how Millais, who was already a master of flowing outline, became stiff and mannered, as in the picture of *Lorenzo and Isabella*, and in order to be unsophisticated, submitted himself to the influence of early monkish drawings and illuminations.

It would not be just to say that Madox Brown originated the Pre-Raphaelite School—it was all in the air. There was a strong feeling of revolt against the insincerity of English art; and if he had not fired the train, it would have been fired by some other hand.

Rossetti gradually drew away from his earlier style; the archaic handling, the stiff treatment of accessories by degrees were left behind. Moreover, he became aware of his limitations. His early training had not been complete. "Proportions," he once said, "always bother me." He said to Mr. Watts-Dunton that Millais's executive power was paralysing to look upon. Breadth of design was another difficulty.

In early days he planned large pictures with much movement and many figures, of which some, like *Cassandra*, remain as designs. Such, too, is *Hist! said Kate the Queen*, a small picture founded on the scheme of a more ambitious one. Some of them were eventually completed on a small scale, such as *The Salutation of Beatrice, Dante drawing the Angel, Dante's Dream, Mary Magdalene at the Door of Simon*, and some few others. But a variety of influences gradually turned his mind in a definite direction. Partly, perhaps, it was the indolence from which he described himself as constitutionally suffering; he was indolent, not lazy. He was a hard and regular worker; but when he had his choice of work, he could not take up what he felt to be difficult. Partly, too, the exigencies of money-making determined him, as his purchasers generally desired the kind of pictures that were supposed to be more typical of his genius. Whatever the causes may have been, he began to devote himself to small pictures without any particular depth of space or action, such as the two pictures *Hamlet and Ophelia*, one of which is a pen and ink drawing, the other a water-colour, and entirely different in treatment, *Bonifazio's Mistress*, *Borgia*, *Paolo and Francesca*, *The Merciless Lady*—pictures in which some dramatic moment is seized upon. Then he began to settle down into the production of the single-figure pictures, of which Mr. Watts-Dunton wrote that "apart from any question of technical shortcomings, one of Rossetti's strongest claims to the attention of posterity was that of having invented, in the three-quarter-length pictures painted from one face, a type of female beauty which was akin to none other,—which was entirely new, in short,—and which, for wealth of sublime and mysterious suggestion, unaided by complex dramatic design, was unique in the art of the world."

This gradual shifting of tendency was, of course, more complex than can be precisely indicated, and it is additionally complicated by Rossetti's frequent production of replicas of early works, or uncompleted designs,—as, for instance, when he took up in 1872 a background of quiet woods and grass fields painted at Sevenoaks in 1850, put in two women playing on musical instruments in the foreground, a castle tower with an open gallery on the right, and two dancing figures in the centre, and named it *The Bower Meadow*.

He was, of course, primarily a colourist, and in water-colour painting especially he produced effects that have never been equalled. The pure glow of colour, fearlessly and prodigally lavished, the daring contrasts, are his own. In 1865 he made the following interesting avowal of his colour preferences:—

"Thinking in what order I love colours, found the following: (1) pure light warm green, (2) deep gold colour, (3) certain tints of grey, (4) shadowy or steel blue, (5) brown, with crimson tinge, (6) scarlet. Other colours (comparatively) only lovable according to the relations in which they are placed." He threw contemptuously aside all the code of rules about the exact proportions of colour to be observed which had held good before his day. What he felt on the subject of colour appears in an interesting letter written to McCracken in 1854:—"I believe colour to be a quite indispensable quality in the *highest* art, and that no picture ever belonged to the highest order without it; while many, by possessing it—as the works of Titian —are raised certainly into the highest *class*, though not to the very highest grade of that class, in spite of the limited degree of their other great qualities. Perhaps the *only* exception which I should be inclined to admit exists in the works of Hogarth, to which I should never dare to assign any but the very highest place, though their colour is certainly not a prominent feature in them. I must add, however, that Hogarth's colour is seldom other than pleasing to myself, and that for my own part, I should almost call him a colourist, though not aiming at colour. On the other hand, there are men who, merely on account of bad colour, prevent me from thoroughly enjoying their works, though full of other qualities. For instance, Wilkie, or Delaroche (in nearly all his works, though the *Hémicycle* is fine in colour). From Wilkie I would at any time prefer a thoroughly good engraving — though of course he is in no respect even within hail of Hogarth. Colour is the physiognomy of a picture; and, like the shape of the human forehead, it cannot be perfectly beautiful without proving goodness and greatness. Other qualities are its life exercised; but this is the body of its life, by which we know and love it at first sight."

Neither was he afraid, in water-colour, of high lights, and let the white paper show in such effects, for instance, as the breaking of sunlight through the thick leaves of a wood, where many painters of his date would have indicated it by superimposed white. Intensity of colour he would have, and one who has often watched him at work has told me that, in days before moist colour was in use, he has seen Rossetti impatiently rub the cake of pigment on the picture to obtain a requisite brilliancy of tone. Ruskin, in the *Art of England*, says that Rossetti was much affected by studying the effects of illuminated MSS., and that the light of his pictures is often such fallen light as comes through stained glass; but this would only apply to certain rich, dim pictures, where he seems to have aimed at a species of twilight effect, as in the beautiful water-colour (1867), a replica of an earlier cartoon, of *Sir Tristram and La Belle Yseult drinking the Love Potion.* They stand in a dark deck-cabin, their heads outlined against a space of breezy sunlit air and bright deck, with a magical light welling from the opened vial on the table between them.

He was fond of painting effects of artificial light —Tibullus returning to Delia, with the lamp lit at evening, and the picture of Dr. Johnson at the Mitre, where the lantern, which is being trimmed by the waiter, struggles with a golden sunrise without, below which lights twinkle in blue house-fronts.

In his technical methods he formed certain habits of a very definite kind, and it must be said that he considered himself primarily an oil-painter, and that only commissions for water-colours had induced him to adopt that medium. He wrote to this effect to the *Athenæum* in 1865, when a statement had been published that he had abandoned oil-painting. He had a very carefully mixed palette for oil-painting, which took nearly an hour to set out before beginning work, and had to be entirely cleaned every evening. All the later half-lengths were done in the same way: after the design was completed, it was drawn in thick red chalk on the canvas, and then the whole was covered with thick white paint mixed with copal varnish, so that the outline glimmered dimly through. The flesh was laid in a monochrome of ultramarine, which produced a peculiar grey shadow. Then, when the stiff white paint had dried, he carefully painted in from the life.

It has been often said that he had but one type of

head, but this is a patent error. He painted from some fourteen models in all. His wife's face was the first type he followed, and then the face of Mrs. Morris and several others, as Mrs. Schott, Miss Ford, Miss Miller, and Miss Spartali, afterwards Mrs. Stillman. But the mannerisms which grew upon him were those of the full lips and the long neck. I have seen three heads in chalk drawn from the same model at different dates, and it is curious to see how the exaggeration grows. The first is normal, and exquisitely beautiful; in the second the lips begin to protrude and the neck to lengthen; in the last the lips have become almost like a butterfly with curved wings settled on the face, and the neck is sinuous, as the neck of a swan. But criticism was impossible; he would have resented it and not have profited by it.

As he grew older he lost to a certain extent the art of hand and eye; but the imagination and the mystical passion of expression, if anything, increased.

Rossetti's pictures fall into several distinct classes:—
The mediæval religious pictures, such as *The Girlhood of Mary Virgin*, the *Ecce Ancilla*, and the centre of the David Triptych. The purely mediæval pictures, rich in colour, such as *King Arthur's Tomb*, *Sir Galahad*, *The Blue Closet*, *The Christmas Carol*, *Before the Battle*. The whole Dante series. The small pictures representing some dramatic emotion, such as *The Laboratory*, *How they met Themselves*, *Paolo and Francesca*, *The Merciless Lady*, *The Madness of Ophelia*, the two pictures called *Lucrezia Borgia*, *Bonifazio's Mistress*, the two pictures of *Hamlet and Ophelia*. Then there are the *genre* pictures, like *Dr. Johnson*, *Found*, *Washing Hands*, and

The Gate of Memory. Then the symbolical pictures of single female figures, to which class most of the later great pictures belong; and these again fall into two classes—those in which some tranquil and happy emotion is displayed, as in *The Beloved, Joli Cœur, The Loving Cup, The Day-Dream, Fiammetta, Bocca Baciata,* and *Belcolore,* and those in which the emotion is of a mystical type, such as *Beata Beatrix, Pandora, Proserpine, Lilith, Veronica Veronese, Regina Cordium, Aurea Catena, Astarte Syriaca,* and *La Pia.* Besides these there are pictures which cannot be exactly classified, such as the strange design of *The Sphinx,* which has a distinct reminiscence of Ingres, the great design for *Cassandra,* and others. There are also many portraits like those of his mother and sister and himself, Browning, Mr. Swinburne, and the Miss Siddal series. There are cartoons and woodcuts.

A few words may be said of these in detail. The early mediæval pictures have a great charm of their own, but are perhaps too distinctly of the nature of a reversion to a certain period of art. The stiff, decorative gestures, the naive grouping, the wealth of mediæval accessory—all seeming to yearn after a simpler and graver manner of life and thought. As James Smetham, a strange, enthusiastic being, said, writing of the *Wedding of St. George,* "one of the grandest things, like a golden dim dream. Love 'credulous all gold,'[1] gold armour, a sense of secret enclosure in 'palace-chambers far apart'; but quaint chambers in quaint palaces, where angels creep in through sliding-panel doors, and stand behind rows of

[1] Quoted from Milton's translation of Horace, *Odes,* I. 5. Smetham slightly misapprehended the meaning of the line.

flowers, drumming on golden bells, with wings crimson and green."

One feels that Rossetti was slowly, as it were, finding his way through this exotic kind of art to the true expression of his personality. Perhaps it was partly that before he had fully learned his limitations, conscious of the great difficulty which the rendering of common things seen in the ordinary light of day presented to one impatient of technical training and eager for expression, he took refuge in these earlier and more simple effects of colour and design. He had not the facility of Millais or the patience of Mr. Holman Hunt. The *Ecce Ancilla Domini* is an attempt to present the scene more naturally. But in *Found* he realised his limitations, and great as the picture is both in conception and partially in execution, the contemplated alterations proved impossible; and he wisely forbore to saddle his genius with conditions with which he could not deal. Perhaps the most elaborate of all these pictures, *Fra Pace*, may be described more in detail.

This picture, a water-colour, was completed in 1856, and was at first in the possession of William Morris. It is worth the closest study, as it stands rather apart from all Rossetti's work, and is a salient instance of how his work might have developed if he had not been drawn by circumstances into the adoption of a settled manner.

It represents a monk kneeling at a desk and making an illumination. The room in which he is at work is a kind of bedroom studio. Above the bed hangs a bell, the rope of which goes down through a large opening in the floor, by which the room seems to be entered, and which gives a glimpse of a tiled passage below and a bit of landscape. The picture is full of abundance of quaint detail, somewhat archaic in character. On the side of the monk's desk hangs a little row of bottles of pigment; on the window-ledge is a dead mouse, which he is drawing; close to his hand lies a slice of pomegranate, also probably serving as a model. On the tail of the monk's frock lies a cat asleep, and a cheerful little acolyte, with a mirthful smile, in a religious dress with embroidered collar and cuffs, is tickling it with a straw. But the charm of the picture is the face of the monk, thin and amiable, with sparse hair, the lips drawn up in the nicety of the work, the quiet eyelid falling over the eye, as he looks downward at his slender brush, held in a strong white hand. There is a tired half-smile on his face, but his complete absorption, together with the ordered look of the quiet room, with its signs of peaceful habitation, strike the note of cloistered calm and tranquil happiness.

Rossetti never entirely deserted the Dante series; these pictures have a character of their own. They are formal in treatment, but not strictly mediæval; there is an attempt to combine a certain freedom of movement with a depth of grouping and dramatic emotion with which he could not wholly cope. The effect that they leave upon the mind is that the pictures are not duly subordinated to some central interest; each figure, each portion of the picture seems in turn as you regard it to be the centre of the composition. They culminated in the *Dante's Dream* of 1870, which is considered by some to be his greatest picture, but which, massive, profound, and learned, in a sense, as it is, fails somehow to bring one very close to the innermost personality of the man.

Then come a number of pictures, mostly small water-colours, in which, though the handling is of a formal character, the stiffness of the more purely mediæval designs is lost, as he gradually acquired a more secure mastery of his art. In such pictures there are generally but a few figures, and some moment of dramatic emotion is seized upon. Such is the *Merciless Lady*, where a man sits in a little arbour looking out on woods, listening to the singing of a light-minded fairy-like maiden, utterly lost in the elfin charm of the soulless, childish grace, while his true love, with her face full of trouble, holds his listless hand, with hatred of her rival and grief at her own loss written legibly in the face. Such again is the *Borgia* of 1851. She sits languidly touching a lute, in an embroidered gown. The evil Pope Alexander VI. leans with a heavy, sensual look over her shoulder; her brother Cæsar stands on the left, beating time upon the table and blowing the rose-leaves from her hair. In the foreground, to the music, dance two children, a boy and a girl. The girl's face is full of a self-conscious charm, but looks as if corruption was entering into her spirit. The boy behind her moves gracefully, with crossed arms, watching the movements of the child, with an innocent face. The pathos of the scene is the thought of what these pretty children are doing in such a place; and to what a bitter end the pursuit of seeming sweet pleasure may come, typified by the dark and marred faces behind.

An interesting pair of pictures of this kind to compare are the two *Hamlets* of 1858 and 1866. In the first, a pen and ink drawing, there is energy and passion in Hamlet's face, as he cries out his contempt for himself with his arms flung wide; but Ophelia, tendering his letters to him with a stiff gesture, her head turned away, is neither natural nor effective. The accessories are all of the most elaborate kind; the scene is laid in an odd nook of carved wooden seats. The carving is curiously designed—a tree of knowledge, encircled with a crowned serpent, and Uzzah falling lifeless from contact with the Ark—indicating doubtless, as by a parable, the perils of too close a contact with the guarded secrets of God; behind is a strange serpentine staircase with double curves leading to a parapet. There is a want of balance about the conception, and the dramatic situation is blurred by the insistence on bizarre detail; but in the later picture, a water-colour, the detail is gone, and we are brought close to the passion of the scene. The two stand in a gallery; he has caught her hand in both of his, and presses it to his lips, his face full of dark brooding; she cannot bear to look him in the face, and a dim and hopeless sorrow, too desperate for tears, is written on her brow.[1]

Then there are a few distinctly *genre* pictures, such as *Dr. Johnson at the Mitre*, and *Found*, which is one of Rossetti's greatest pictures. It was designed about 1851, and he was working at it in 1854. But it was never completed, though commissioned by three or four successive purchasers. It represents a drover in the early morning driving a cart into London which contains a calf confined by a net. Near a bridge he finds

[1] This picture was not originally intended to represent Hamlet and Ophelia, but merely the parting of two lovers.

crouching on the pavement his early love, in the last stage of a life of degradation; he tries to lift her up, but she crouches away from him in abasement. The picture is full of fine symbolism, but the perspective of the bridge, and the very stones of the street, which might have been dealt with in Rossetti's earlier years, were impossibilities for him when he had lost the power, which he never possessed in any great degree, of painting in the open air. And the difficulties were increased by the fact that he thought the figures, as originally drawn, too short, and determined at a later date to lengthen them.

There is left that strange series of beautiful half-length female figures, which to most people are all that is meant in art by the name of Rossetti. These are of two very distinct types: the simpler type represents a sweet, untroubled, natural beauty, a beauty that is indeed a rare flower of life, and to the development of which would seem to have gone a freedom from care, months and years of seemly and guarded life, unruffled by anxiety and unshadowed by passion, desiring nothing out of measure. Such are the beautiful *Belcolore, Bocca Baciata, The Loving Cup, Joli Cœur*, and others. The proudest and sweetest of all is *Fiammetta*, who steps out with a radiant motion from the fresh apple-blossoms, the very spirit of lustrous youth, saved only from insolence by utter charm. These gracious creatures look out at the gazer with a tranquil and unconscious air of maiden thought, knowing nothing of the deeper shadows of life, of pain, and doom; there is no mystery about their days; they are like Nausicaa and Shirley, surrounded by the silent worship of gentle persons; they have "but fed on the roses and lain in the lilies of life."

But of the rest it is hard to speak, because the emotions they arouse are so intangible, so remote, that they pass beyond the reach of words. With some of them, indeed, one feels as if their mind was set on evil, as though they were determined to feed the flame of their desire with all delicate things in earth and heaven. Such is the *Venus Verticordia*, the perfection of the beauty that is merely of the body, with the unashamed glance beneath the drooping lids; such is *Lilith*, with her cold, strong face, shadowed by her hair, the room all flooded with roses and light. Such is *La Bella Mano*, for all the wistful innocence of her winged ministers. Such in a darker mood are the crayons, *The Lady with the Fan*, and the *Aurea Catena*, where the beauty cannot struggle out of the shade of sombre thought. Darker and deeper still is the *Astarte Syriaca*, robed in the green of a shoaling sea, with silver girdle, looking out of a blood-red sky, where the struggling moon is veiled. Here, indeed, the two attendants, with their torches and upward glance, seem to testify to some dark, unholy power, the cruelty that is akin to lust. The strange sights that she has seen in grove and shrine seem to have fed her beauty with a lurid and terrible royalty, where she reigns in a dark serenity which nothing can appal.

Then there is the *Sea-Spell*, with the barbarous harp, the very spirit of Nature's careless music, the piping of shrill winds, the moan of inarticulate waves. With this is associated the graceful *Veronica Veronese*, the nymph of earthly music, who, with the languid air of one who pursues an impossible dream, seems to desire to translate the shrill bird's song into the language of the tense string.

But there are three pictures of this class that leave the deepest impression in the mind. One is the *Proserpine*, the picture that was wrought through such a series of calamities. Deeply mannerised though it is, the face has in it the proud bearing of irreparable doom, the empire of sorrow that has become a part of life; that cannot touch the radiance of divine beauty, but has left its mark in the eyes that seem to be as dark wells into which all the pain of the world has streamed.

Another is *Pandora*, with her metal casket from which the red smoke streams. She seems to be rather the spirit of terror incarnate; she is a beautiful witch who has seen all that the world holds of fear, and has yet divined what is august and awe-inspiring in terror, casting from her all the meaner attributes, all shrinking cowardice and craven dismay.

But perhaps the noblest of all these heads is the *Beata Beatrix*, of which Rossetti himself said that no picture ever cost him so much pain in painting, but at the same time he had never been more conscious of mastery in art.[1] The face is his wife's; and it was the first time after her death that he allowed himself to recall it. It is the symbol of the death of the body, " not," as he said, "intended at all to represent death, but to render it under the semblance of a trance in which . . . she is suddenly rapt from earth to heaven." It is one of the pictures of Rossetti's where the subordination is perfect. The dial, the listening figures behind, the crimson dove, divert no

[1] There are no known studies for the *Beata Beatrix*. The supposed studies are later. He probably used some studies made for *The Return of Tibullus*.

pleased attention from the upturned face, with the soft, golden light playing over the waxen features from which life seems withdrawn. But there is no threatening of mortality to mar the vision, and the face is the face of one whose heart's desire is fulfilled beyond the reach of hope.

A few words may be said about his work in illustrating books. Some dozen such illustrations exist in all. One is an illustration for W. Allingham's *Day and Night Songs*, 1855. Five appear in the illustrated Tennyson published by Moxon in 1857, and four appear in two books by his sister Christina, *Goblin Market* and *The Prince's Progress*, published in 1862 and 1866.

The Tennyson illustrations are the most interesting, especially that for the *Lady of Shalott*, where Lancelot, pale and sad, bends down from a stairway descending on the river to the barge, where the maiden lies under a wooden hooding bearing lighted candles; but the design is crowded, and it is lacking in contrast and airy quality. Much the most carefully finished one is that to the *Palace of Art*, an extraordinarily intricate design full of little incidents that have no existence in the poem. St. Cecily kneels at an organ with hands laid on the keys, with the head thrown back in the embrace of a strange, wild figure more pilgrim than angel. The scene is laid in a beleaguered city guarded and mounted with cannon, and a sea in the background crowded with great ships. In the foreground is a soldier eating an apple as he guards a dungeon on the platform of which kneels the saint.

Of this picture Rossetti humorously wrote that he was going to try a subject "where one can allegorize on one's own hook on the subject of the poem, without killing for oneself and every one a distinct idea of the poet's."

In the illustrations to his sister's poems there is much charm, particularly in the picture *Buy from us with a golden curl*, where the girl clips a lock of her hair to pay for the fruits brought by the odd creatures of the wood. There is a great deal of humour in the sly, wheedling looks of the grotesque animals, especially in the solemn fish which tries to press in at the back, and the strange cub-like creature in the foreground, in a species of sleepy ecstasy.

Perhaps the most beautiful of all is the frontispiece, etched, but fastidiously rejected, for *The Early Italian Poets* (1861). This picture, representing a kneeling lover, whose lady bends to kiss him, gives, with simple lines, the effect of the purest emotion entirely removed from any sensuous association.

Rossetti was one of those natures which are entirely dominated and penetrated by the beauty of the world, and his whole life was devoted to the expression of this haunting and almost torturing consciousness. I do not think that there is any evidence that he looked upon himself as an interpreter or prophet of beauty to others; and one of the many mysteries of his strange life is the fact that he possessed such a curious power over the lives and minds of others, without apparently having any desire to exert this influence. It seems never to have been consciously exerted even over those within his immediate circle; as for those without, I do not imagine that he regarded them at all. He lived in the spirit of Horatian thought—

> "Odi profanum vulgus et arceo;
> Favete linguis! carmina non prius
> Audita Musarum sacerdos
> Virginibus puerisque canto."

The *virgines puerique* of Rossetti's audience were all those who could look past the sordid pursuits of the world and keep their eye steadily fixed on beauty in her inmost shrine.

But it was for Rossetti one special form of beauty that thus stung and overpowered his spirit. Just as in the case of Morris it was the love of the kindly and gracious earth, as to Browning it was the complicity and grandeur of human motive, as to Mr. Holman Hunt it has been a stern sense of the Divine, to Rossetti it was the beauty of the human face, as the sublimest form of loveliness that the dreaming spirit of nature could conceive. Earth and the things of earth touched him only as sweet accessories to this central beauty, the purest, fairest, and divinest thing that the earth can hold.

But this beauty is not, as Rossetti understood it, an end in itself; it is not the sense of desirous possession that is stirred by it, but rather it is a deep-seated thirst for the mystery, whatever it may be, that hides beneath and beyond it. It is the beauty that brings with it awe and reverence and honour, and a sense of kinship with immortal and everlasting things, not dwelling on the figure but the face.

I imagine that there is something of the same feeling in the minds of the most exalted moralists. What draws them to virtue is not a philosophical, reasoned sense of the merits of virtue and its usefulness in compacting the framework of life into stability and serviceableness. It is rather the haunting passion of the *beauty* of virtue of which Wordsworth speaks in the *Ode to Duty*:—

> "Nor know we anything so fair
> As is the smile upon thy face."

A noble deed, a splendid piece of self-sacrifice, a triumph of justice over tyranny—these have the same constraining attractiveness for the highest souls that beauty has for the artist; they are all messages from some distant fortress of God, from some abstract city built on foundations of amethyst and with gates of pearl. Such a passion for virtue cannot be learned, hardly instilled; though those in whom it exists in a dim and imperfect form may by faithful effort learn to imitate what at first they only half-heartedly admire.

Thus we should welcome gladly among us the advent and passage of all clear-sighted souls, who live not, as others live, for the moment, but under the dominion of some high and eternal idea. We may think that the passion for what is beautiful in conduct is the highest range of which the human spirit is capable, and we may regret the devotion to an art which does not end in the ennobling of human character. But who could say that those who live laboriously faithful to the pure vision of beauty in art do not tend to the uplifting of the human spirit higher? It may not be, as Myers wrote, so "manifestly akin to virtue"; but anything deserves praise which is a protest against materialism, against gross and animal views of life, against the seductions of comfort, against all limited satisfaction. I would claim for Rossetti's art that it is essentially of this kind. It does not aim at satisfying, and surely it is an incredible view which would see in it a merely sensual outlook. Sensuous it may be, nay, is bound to be, because it is the very strangeness and mystery of love that the passion which is most remote in its significance, most enthralling in its suddenness, which brings a touch of divineness into the most brutish life, should be so inextricably interwoven with the fiercest assaults of the animal nature.

But it is to no mere love-dalliance, no temporary thrill of pleasure, no gross vehemence of passion which drinks and passes on ungrateful and heedless, to which these strange and dreamful visions of Rossetti call us. They draw us rather to that strange sense of haunting desire which is, as it were, so incommunicable in essence that it can only be expressed in types and hints and far-off dreams. Those who know the inexpressible thrill which invades the mind at the sight of some dewy wood-end seen from an opened casement in the silent freshness of dawn, or the thickening tide of twilight, when the wood stands black against the green depth of sky; or the sight of the secret glade, muffled in leaves, and carpeted, as by some sweet conspiracy, with the drooping sweetness of spring hyacinths; or who have watched the twilight flying and flaring to the west over miles of quiet country, when the mind asks itself what is the strange and blissful secret that it seems upon the verge of guessing—it is to these that the faces that look so sorrowfully, so seriously out of the pictures of

Rossetti, speak. It is not even the frank and childish appetite of seeing the thing beautifully portrayed which we can win from these pictures; the least critical can see the lack of mastery, the mannerism, the want of draughtsmanship, under the magnificence of colour that they display. Rossetti was too intent upon setting forth his visions to master the technical secrets of painting.

It may be said that all this kind of art is essentially outside experience and therefore unwholesome. Such is the argument of the conventional man, the Philistine, the Roman, and to that it can only be replied that those on whom such pictures of Rossetti's exercise no attractive and dreamful quality will do best to leave them alone. They will not reveal their charm to the inquisitive. Neither, again, should we sympathise with the spirit that found its ultimate satisfaction in such art as this. The region of the dreamer is a dangerous one in which to linger; in the old stories it would befall the man who loved to wander alone on trackless hills to see suddenly some strange vision which unfitted him to return to the common life of man, while at the same time he could find no words to tell what it was that had visited his sight. It sent him forth to wander unsatisfied and haggard in lonely places; and this loneliness, this remoteness, is the danger of all who yield themselves too recklessly to the pursuit and contemplation of the mystery which lends little inner happiness to the spirit. But, on the other hand, to be blind to this kind of beauty is to be blind to an undoubted and potent vision; it is to be materialistic, to be limited, to be heedless of the huge secrets that lie all about us on every hand. To heed them, to follow them warily, to love them is not to be unmanly, or slothful, or vague, so long as these emotions do not absorb, but quicken and elevate the soul.

There are two totally distinct views of Art: one that would regard it, in whatever form it comes, as an agreeable accessory to life and no more—"after the banquet the minstrel"; that is the view of the uninitiated, the Philistine, the man in the street, and all those that are without.

But again there is the inner view of those to whom Art is a strange and enchanted country of dreaming woodland, league upon league, with here and there the tower of some haunted abode looking over into the silent glades; here wanders a spirit, finger on lip but with a questioning smile. The story of the place to those who have ever set foot within it seems a foolish tale, like the murmur of the wind or the ripple of the stream, vague and meaningless.

But it is not to be entered heedlessly. It is like the *Woods of Westermain*—

> "Enter these enchanted woods,
>   Ye who dare. . . .
> These, the woods of Westermain,
> Are as others to behold,
> Rich of wreathing sun and rain ;
> Foliage lustreful around
> Shadowed leagues of slumbering sound."

But the head must be cool and the heart clean to walk there without danger; here have perished many strong and beautiful souls; and it were better not to set foot at all within the sunlit glades than to tread carelessly. For though you may return, yet to have tasted of the joys and terrors of the place will unfit you for the simpler life of man; but those who can walk warily can go and come, and bring back fruits like the grapes of Eshcol and star-flowers of Paradise to refresh the wayfarers of the world who may not enter.

CHAPTER VIII

CHARACTER

IN attempting to draw Rossetti's character it is necessary to remember that we are not dealing with an English type at all. It is hard to sketch him in English tones, not only because his temperament was so intricate and many-sided, but from its intensity and force. As Ruskin wrote in *Præterita*, "Rossetti was really not an Englishman, but a great Italian tormented in the Inferno of London." Deepest down lay a mystical passion for the beauty which culminates in the human form, which, like everything else in the man, was not a sentiment but a strong constraining influence. He was strongly susceptible to feminine charm, and had a correspondingly strong influence over women; but to confuse this with mere sensuous impulse would be a grave mistake. To him the forms of human loveliness were in themselves dear and adorable, but they were only, so to speak, the first steps in a shining stairway that led among the stars; they were but the alphabet of a passion whose finished scrolls were written by the very finger of God. It is difficult for English minds adequately to conceive the remote and dimly apprehended possibilities which for Rossetti lay behind material forms of beauty, and to gauge the depth of the secret of which hints were written in the precise forms of hands and lips and eyes.

But side by side with this mystical hunger of the soul, there existed in Rossetti what is not generally found in combination with it. He had an intellectual nature of extraordinary vividness, a hard mental force which gained in strength from the extremely definite limitations of his mind. He took no interest in politics, history, metaphysics, or science, and the whole strength of an acute and penetrating intellect was given to art and poetry. He was contemptuously impatient of talk on such subjects as I have indicated, which were to him utterly barren and arid. Yet those who knew him best always held that the man was infinitely greater than his work, which carelessly and inevitably radiated from him, hurled out from an inner restlessness. The medium in which he worked, whether words or colours, was a hindrance rather than a help to him.

Although his genius was creative rather than imitative, he had a great power of relentless observation— no foible or characteristic in his friends escaped him. He had the same penetrative insight in dealing with books. His library was small, but he valued *quality* in a book above everything. His interest in china, furniture, *objets d'art* was just the same—intensely critical, pungent, sharp-sighted. The same quality came out in the financial ability which he possessed. He had an eye, says Mr. Mackail, for anything with money in it. Though profuse, generous, and extravagant with money, he valued it as a power, as meaning freedom. His income was very considerable, and he displayed the least attractive side of his nature in his acute bargaining. I put this down largely to the restrictions in the matter of money under which he grew to maturity. A haunting sense of poverty in early years is apt to make a generous nature too heedful of gain and to give an exaggerated idea of the necessity of money as an accessory to life.

It is impossible to insist too strongly on a certain element in Rossetti's character which can only be described as a natural kingliness. He had an absolutely dominant nature, not a deep-seated force of will, but a personal dominance. He was master of the moment, of the scene, of the company; every one who encountered him, and he was surrounded by a number of highly original personalities, bowed to this influence. He was the undisputed sovereign of any group in which he found himself. His brother writes: "He was a genial despot, good-naturedly hearty and unassuming in manner and only tenacious upon the question at issue." For the sake of his affection and generosity his friends forgave him a great deal of inconsiderateness in details, which was very characteristic of his early life. Thus Madox Brown's journal for the end of 1854 gives an incisive picture of Rossetti, who was supposed to be painting *Found*. In the course of November Rossetti was quartered at Finchley, where Brown was then living in considerable poverty with his wife, who was expecting her confinement. Brown says pathetically that Rossetti sleeps in their parlour, a bed being made up on the floor, and will not get up till eleven o'clock; that he makes very slow progress with the calf, painting hair by hair, "all the time he wearing my great-coat, which I want, and a pair of my breeches"; requiring unlimited supplies of food and turpentine, and quite impervious to hints that his presence was inconvenient. "I told him delicately he must go, or go home at night by the 'bus. This he said was too expensive. I told him he might ride to his work in the morning, and walk home at night. This he said he should never think of."

These extracts bring out very strongly both the inconsiderate self-will of Rossetti, and his apparent indifference to the convenience of others. It can hardly have been want of perception, but I suppose was rather an intense and self-absorbed pre-occupation in his own work and thoughts. Still more remarkable is the fact that Madox Brown seems not to have resented it, hardly to have questioned Rossetti's right to behave as he did. He prays for deliverance, as from the will of some peremptory monarch, rather than asserts his equality and social rights.

This magnetism dominated Morris absolutely for a time, it determined the art of Burne-Jones, it upset Ruskin, it profoundly affected Mr. Swinburne's poetry. His influence was not consciously exerted; it is a mistake to think of Rossetti as a proselytiser. He laid no snares for other natures; but in his presence his conceptions and aims naturally presented themselves to others as the conceptions and aims most worth striving for. He was intensely affectionate, a loyal friend, an irresistible comrade. He took no account of anything but the charm and enthusiasm of the character he was brought into contact with, so that for him social distinctions did not exist. He never conceived himself bound to sympathise with another point of view—indeed the possibility of doing so did not enter his mind; when he said a thing, *it was to be.* " I was one of those," he once wrote, "whose little is their own." This directness of energy, combined with the fact that he was also strangely and wonderfully attractive in himself, had an irresistible power over other minds, above all, over minds in search of an ideal.

The cause, I think, of so many broken friendships in his life was not, as has been suggested, Rossetti's own capriciousness, nor the morbidity of his later years, nor even the sad circumstances of his life. It was rather that his friends were often men of strong individuality, such as Morris, Ruskin, and others, and that they felt themselves overpowered and dominated by Rossetti in a way which made easy intercourse difficult and uncomfortable. As Madox Brown, writing after Rossetti's death, said, "I find now what I was scarcely conscious of before, that I used to paint always with a vague idea of his approbation in the distance." There were not, as a rule, any sharp and definite ruptures of friendship; it was rather that his associates felt themselves in the presence of a man whose strength of will overpowered and overwhelmed their own marked characteristics, and expected a natural submission which they were not prepared to concede, which might be borne for a time while they were under the spell, but which was bound to cease in the natural course of development. His friends were as a rule originally attracted to Rossetti by his powerful charm; but close and intimate alliances between men of very salient and marked characteristics seldom stand the strain of prolonged association. Those friends who remained faithful to Rossetti were mostly men of gentler mould, who did not run counter to his preferences and prejudices, and who remained under the fascination of his generous and enthusiastic personality, without wishing to assert themselves.

There is something very remarkable in the spectacle presented by the closing years. Rossetti appears surrounded by what was almost a little court of followers, who laid out their time to suit him, came to him at times when he desired to have company, and cheerfully sacrificed their own convenience to serve his needs. He appears hardly to have appreciated this to the full, though these devoted friends seem to have been amply repaid by the royal and generous recognition of their services which he from time to time rendered them. Something of a tragic pity for the doom under which their hero lay, perhaps imparted a deeper quality to this devotion. Many a man in Rossetti's position, morbid, self-indulgent, wilfully pursuing his own way reckless of consequences, would have been sternly abandoned to his own devices; but the glimpses that one gets of the later years in the pages of Mr. William Rossetti's book have something that is singularly impressive and touching. The object of their devotion lies ill and indifferent, under the spell of a terrible drug, impatient of pain, while the faithful friends in sad conclave make arrangements for his comfort, select a place for his retreat, settle the relays of vigilant and untiring companions to accompany him, disregard their own occupations, with an entire unconsciousness that they are displaying any marked degree of self-sacrifice.

"What a supreme man is Rossetti!" wrote Philip Bourke Marston, the blind poet, in 1873. "Why is he not some great exiled king, that we might give our lives in trying to restore him to his kingdom?"

This was exactly the spirit in which his friends did serve him. It is like the story of some dethroned monarch, surrounded by adherents who make the misfortunes of their leader a reason for lavishing on him the care and devotion which they would hardly have conceded to him if he had been prosperous and regnant. This is not the spirit of a coterie, but something of a much larger and deeper kind, based on a consciousness of the man's greatness and natural royalty.

Mr. Gosse, who as a very young man was introduced into the circle, says that the personal impressiveness of Rossetti can hardly be exaggerated. The difficulties in the way of seeing him, the secrecy preserved about his pictures, so that it was possible to be a frequent visitor to the house and yet rarely to be allowed to visit the studio, all enhanced the air of mystery. But the man himself, short, stout, careless in dress, unaffected in discourse, seemed yet to carry with him a certain pontifical greatness, as though he were the very high-priest of beauty, and held the key to the innermost mysteries of art. "And all this," as Mr. Gosse wrote, "without a single touch of the prophetic manner, the air of such professional seers as Coleridge or Carlyle." This sense was enhanced and not diminished by the entire absence of æsthetic pretence, by Rossetti's simple manners and easy, indifferent habits, by the rich, resonant voice, which aroused an almost physical vibration in his hearers.

This personal dominance was sustained by the splendid appreciation which he always showed of the work of others. He had not a particle of jealousy in his composition; and the lavish commendation which he was always ready to bestow upon the artistic productions of friends and rivals was one of the sources of his influence. There is, indeed, in these early days, abundant evidence of small, troublesome, detailed kindnesses, lavished upon his friends with a profusion which a selfish character could never have attained to. He takes an editor and a leading contributor of a weekly to see a friend's pictures; he writes a long article in the same paper pointing out the merits of the pictures in question; he brings possible purchasers half across London to see the same; or, a picture in an exhibition by an unknown man strikes him as having merit; he insists that a moneyed friend should buy it; he secures a good notice for it in the *Times*; he takes Ruskin to see it. As Ford Madox Brown, in a time of great discouragement, wrote: "Really Gabriello seems bent upon making my fortune at one blow. Never did fellow, I think, so bestir himself for a rival before; it is very good and very great to act so." And again :—

"No one ever perhaps showed such a vehement disposition to proclaim any real merit if he thinks he discovers it in an unknown or rising artist. . . . I could narrate a hundred instances of the most noble and disinterested conduct towards his art-rivals, which places him far above [others] in his greatness of soul, and yet he will, on the most trivial occasion, hate and backbite any one who gives him offence."

To the very end of his life, says one who knew him well, nothing was more remarkable than the attention he was always prepared to give to the artistic and literary work of unknown men. William Morris, in the later years of estrangement, is said to have held that Rossetti's deepest fault of character was his unalloyed selfishness; but William Morris had always been far more absorbed in his own pursuits than Rossetti was, and treated the work of others, unless it were of a kind that specially appealed to himself, with unconcealed impatience. Rossetti, on the contrary, was almost invariably ready, except in a whimsical mood, to consider a picture or a poem respectfully, to praise its merits, to criticise helpfully, even to alter and amend, if he could; and this characteristic never deserted him.

There was, too, no tendency to condescension about him; he did not think of his own prestige, but put any young man, in whom he discerned loftiness of aim and high artistic intention, on a level with himself and other experienced workers.

Together with this was a readiness to give advice, absorbed as he was in his own work, on any matter in which he felt he could be of use. To give one out of many such instances, there is preserved an early letter, full of practical sense and kindliness, to his aunt, who had asked his advice as to how to begin to teach drawing to a small class of entirely unpractised amateurs. He suggests the minute copying of a piece of mossy bark, in pencil and then in colour; he offers to look over the result and criticise, to procure suitable casts for models and materials, and to send them. All this is very different from the moody seclusion of later years, self-absorbed and irresolute. But we must again and again remind ourselves that the latter was not the real Rossetti. Even then, weakened and enslaved as he was by his pernicious habit, he was for ever accessible to any personal appeal that could penetrate his seclusion, and apt to discharge offices of tenderness and solicitude for any of the narrowing circle that surrounded him.

What throws a beautiful light upon Rossetti's character is the profound tenderness and filial devotion which he displayed to his mother throughout his life. His letters to her, of which many are published, have a sweetness and a deliberate cheerfulness that show not only how deeply rooted his affection was, but what capacities for self-sacrificing loyalty there lay in his nature. He addressed her often in odd pet names of his own devising: "Good Antique," "Dear good Antique," "Dear old Darling of 70," "Dearest Darling," and so forth. And such letters as the following show the nature of the tie that bound them:—

". . . I have only got your letter this morning. It would be absurd in me to thank you for another proof of the affection which you have lavished on me all my life, and which is often but too little deserved. I am most ashamed of my disgraceful silence all the time I have been at Oxford; but I am getting worse than ever as a letter-writer, though this should hardly apply in your dear case."

"*May* 12, 1868.

"The reminder of the solemn fact that I am a man of forty now could hardly come agreeably from any one but yourself. But, considering that the chief blessing of my forty good and bad years has been that not one of them has taken you from me, it is the best of all things to have the same dear love and good wishes still coming to me to-day from your dear hand at a distance as they would have done from your dear mouth had we seen each other. This we shall again soon, I trust."

"PENKILL, 1868.

"GOOD ANTIQUE,— . . . I have just got your dear letter, and one from William. In yours I think I detect a funny old intention of writing large for the benefit of my sight. This would be quite in the Antique spirit."

It was the same with the other members of his family. The long series of letters to his brother William show the fraternal relation at its best; they are absolutely natural and simple, but there is none of the gruffness or curtness which often creeps into fraternal communications. Thus he wrote to his brother in 1872, after his recovery from the saddest of his illnesses:—

"I know well how much you must have suffered on my account; indeed perhaps your suffering may have been more acute than my own dull nerveless state during the past months. Your love, dear William, is not less returned by me than it is sweet to me, and that is saying all."

From the first there was in the family circle a habit of outspoken and impulsive affection which was characteristic of their Italian origin. I cannot refrain from quoting a letter written at an early date to D. G. Rossetti by his father, which shows that the affection of the household was not left unexpressed, to be taken for granted, as is perhaps not unusual among English families. The letter runs:—

"FROME, 4*th October* 1853.

"For some while past I have been feeling a strong impulse to write to you, my dearly beloved son; and to-day I will obey this imperious inner voice. . . .

"I am extremely pleased at the progress which you are making in your beautiful art, and at some profits which you are earning from it to maintain yourself with decorum in society. Remember, my dearly loved son, that you have only your abilities to rely upon for your welfare. Remember that you were born with a marked propensity, and that, from your earliest years, you made us conceive the brightest hopes that you would become a great painter.

"And such you will be, I am certain. . . ."

It is encouraging and uplifting in dealing with a character like Rossetti's to find the fire of tender affection burn so clear in the innermost sanctuary; it allays the suspicion that self-absorption and artistic pre-occupation had dried up the sources of tenderness. It is profoundly affecting to realise that the pure spring of natural affection ran clear and untainted all through his troubled days, and that he clung to the love of his childish years. Nor was he merely content that this should be lavished upon him. The letters show that he dwelt much upon the thought of his mother, and kept up a constant and regular correspondence with her, as though he had been a boy at school craving for the atmosphere of affection that surrounded him at home. His affection for his friends was only less strong and generous than his affection for his family. He would banter them robustly and unmercifully; but he had an extreme dislike, incisive though his wit was, of giving pain to any one. A letter written to Madox Brown in 1866 reflects a wonderful depth of affection:—

"Nothing, on reflection, could pain me more (though certainly I did so in a way to which I ought not to have been blind) than to inflict the slightest pain on you, whom I regard as so much the most intimate and dearest of my friends, that I might call you by comparison the only one I have. . . . To refer to another point (having said all that seems possible in confession of how much I was to blame), I may say that the suggestion of any possible obligation from you to me seriously distresses me. Not because I think you attribute my thoughtlessness in any degree to such a view on my own part, for of that you acquit me by word as well as I should in any case have known by thought; but because if *you* can disregard, as I know you do, the great obligations under which you have laid me in early life, and which were real ones, as involving real troubles to yourself undertaken for the sake of one who was quite a stranger to you at the outset—what can *I* think of a matter which gives me no trouble whatever, and in which, were I inactive, I should sin against affection, gratitude, and, highest of all, conviction as an artist?"

And again in 1874 he writes to Madox Brown:—

"The better I am, the more intensely I feel your friendship in word and deed. I need not doubt that you have pardoned any feeble petulance of my late ailing condition."

And very characteristic of him it was to make the alteration which he did in the sonnet on the clergyman who destroyed Shakespeare's Mulberry Tree. The concluding lines ran—

"Whose soul is carrion now,—too mean to yield
Some tailor's ninth allotment of a ghost."

He altered the word "tailor" into "Starveling," to the great detriment of the pungency of the allusion, for fear of "hurting the feelings of some sensitive member or members of the tailoring craft who might dislike the line in its original wording."

One other feature of this generosity of character

must be touched upon: his extraordinary liberality and kindness in the matter of material help. In his use of money he had a certain magnificence; and though he was inconsiderate and even unscrupulous when dealing with purchasers, and in some cases with friends in matters of finance, yet the instinct of generosity was unfailing. It mattered not who it was—a friend, an acquaintance, a complete stranger. The pressure of visible distress always appealed instantly to Rossetti's heart. Not only would he give away any money of which he was possessed, but he had no scruple in borrowing from his friends for the same purpose. In early days he was not particular about repayment, and a temporary difference, which was quite erroneously supposed to have arisen between himself and his brother William, was laughingly explained by a friend, who said that William Rossetti was obliged to be careful, as whenever he met his brother he was called upon to produce any available coin that he had upon him. Among innumerable instances of his ready kindness, one will suffice. On reaching home after his wedding tour he heard of the death of a young writer named Brough, who had left a wife and two little children. Rossetti knew that the widow would be practically destitute. He had spent all his own money; but a certain portion had been invested in jewellery for Mrs. Rossetti, who fully sympathised with the trouble in question; so that when they reached London they did not go straight home, but drove first to a pawn-broker, and then to Mrs. Brough's lodgings, and after that home, "with entirely empty pockets; but, I expect," says Arthur Hughes, who tells the story, "with two very full hearts."

A great deal of harm was done to the cause which Rossetti represented, the whole-hearted pursuit of beauty, by the affectations and absurdities introduced, after, and even before, his death, by a group of self-elected followers, the *epigoni* who took up in a self-conscious and superficial way the ideas which were popularly supposed to have actuated his teaching, and used them as a means of gaining notoriety and social distinction. The so-called æsthetic school, satirised in *Punch* under the figures of Postlethwaite and Maudle, were no doubt in a degree sincere. They professed to refer all things to the standard of the Beautiful, but their devotion was tainted partly by the fact that they made these principles an excuse for lowering the moral standard, and partly because they desired above all things *monstrari digito*, to be pointed out as daring innovators and contemners of existing conventions. The result was that the originators of the æsthetic movement were credited with all sorts of affectations which not only formed no part of their scheme, but which were entirely alien to their whole spirit. It cannot, however, be said that the principles of the movement have in any way profoundly affected or influenced the national life and feeling; and the net result of the school, apart from a temporary quickening of the artistic conscience, and an enhancing of the dignity of art, has been of a decorative kind, and has mainly succeeded in raising the general level of domestic taste.

It is a strange instance of the irony of fate that the affectations of unworthy imitators should be charged upon the original founders of the movement. They were rather sedulously unaffected. "I *can't* get on with men who are not men of the world," Rossetti said in 1864 to his brother The Pre-Raphaelites spoke no artistic jargon, but rather preferred a short, crisp, vernacular, slangy vocabulary. "Stunning" was a favourite adjective where their imitators spoke of "precious." Rossetti frequents the British Museum in order to find "stunning words" for poetry, and a friendly waitress at an eating-house was known as the "cordial stunner." Mr. Holman Hunt says that while Rossetti "worthily rejoiced in the poetic atmosphere of the sacred and spiritual dreams that then encircled him," "some of his noisy demonstrations at the time might hinder this from being recognised by a hasty judgment." Rossetti had a taste in talk for strong vernacular expressions. "You'd better collar it," "I expect I cribbed it from her,"—it was thus that he preferred to talk. Rossetti, writing to Allingham in August 1854, says, "I have got out my work this morning, but it looks so hopelessly beastly, and I feel so hopelessly beastly, that I must try to revive myself before beginning, by some exercise that goes quicker than the Fine Arts." Dr. Birkbeck Hill says that he was present at a discussion at Oxford, when Rossetti was engaged upon the Union frescoes, when the latter maintained that a young and lovely woman, who was on her trial on a charge of murdering her lover, ought not to be hanged even if found guilty, because she was "such a stunner!" Mr. Hill took the opposite view. "Oh, Hill," said a now famous painter, "you would never hang a stunner!" Again, Rossetti, writing to Madox Brown in 1861, says: "A few blokes and coves are coming at eight or so on Friday evening to participate in oysters and obloquy. Will you identify yourself with them and their habits?"

Rossetti, indeed, on occasions, could behave with an unconventionality which was almost undignified, but his personal charm was such that he was able to extricate himself from disagreeable situations in which a less good-humoured man might have provoked serious or unpleasant consequences. His behaviour to those in whom he discerned a type of beauty which struck him, was unconventional to the verge of offensiveness and beyond. One of his models made his acquaintance first by finding him running out of a confectioner's with a half-bitten tart in his hand to stare in her face. Another, a simple country girl, felt, as she sat in a restaurant, her hair suddenly seized and untied. She remonstrated very vehemently. "I wanted to see how it looked," was the reply; and a few minutes after, such was his personal fascination, she had made an appointment to sit for a picture. He would call a cabman off his rank with an opprobrious name, and make friends with him on the strength of the insult. He was walking on one occasion with Mr. and Mrs. William Morris at Upton. They happened to pass a village school when the children were singing a hymn. On the conclusion of the performance, Rossetti put his head in at the window and shouted a stentorian *Amen*. The Morrises, as respectable householders, fled in haste, and the irate schoolmistress came out to remonstrate. Yet so potent was Rossetti's personal influence, that in ten minutes he was holding in the schoolroom an extemporised examination in geography, and awarding penny prizes for good answers. But his practical humour in early days had often something perverse and even unscrupulous about it. He made Dean Stanley aghast by excusing elaborately in his presence the vices of Neronian Rome. In all this there was no desire to pose as eccentric. Exasperated by any suspicion of sanctimoniousness, he was merely following the impulse of the moment to a whimsical excess of paradox.

Such slight reminiscences as these indicate that the Brotherhood were above all things unaffected. They were far too much concerned with the spirit of the thing to waste any time in adopting a pose about it. It was so with Rossetti to the end. When he wrote or painted, he threw into both the highest enthusiasm, and surrounded his conceptions with all the dignity conceivable. But he had a great talent for caricature and humorous drawing which he freely employed for the amusement of his friends, and his talk was plain, brisk, sensible, pungent, and vigorous even when he was expressing the deepest mysteries of art. What could be more absolutely unaffected than the following narration of how Ford Madox Brown and Rossetti came to the conclusion that a statue of Bacon on which Woolner was engaged was too short? Brown hinted this to the sculptor, but "fearing he would not [alter it] sufficiently, I proposed to Gabriel that we should go together, and insist upon the head being made smaller and the body longer. Rossetti said he would come, but I must be spokesman, as he funked it. However, while I was looking at the statue and thinking how to begin, Rossetti, who, by the way, had all along before sworn the statue was perfect, blurts out, 'I say, that chap's too short, I certainly think.' In this delicate way he broke the ice, and we began in earnest."

Humour indeed was one of Rossetti's strongest characteristics—not delicate, fanciful, remote humour, but broad, laughable, pungent. In 1850, when he was painting the background of *The Bower-Meadow* down at Sevenoaks with Holman Hunt in rainy weather, he gives a very whimsical account of his troubles. "Hunt gets on swimmingly—yesterday, indeed, a full inch over the ankles: I myself had to sketch under the canopy of heaven, without a hat, and with my umbrella tied over my head to my buttonhole—a position which, will you oblige me by remembering, I expressly desired should be selected for my statue. . . . I saw the back of a pair of top boots, and a cutaway coat; Lord Amherst, I was told, was sneaking inside, but he refrained from exposing either his person or his ideas on Art. His house is visited with artists in Egyptian swarms, poor wretch! Hunt remarked—'How disagreeable to enter one of your rooms for the purpose of delivering a soliloquy, and find a man there behind an easel'; which was bobbish for Hunt."

His talk was still more incisive, and his criticisms relentlessly humorous. For instance, he said of William Morris that "Topsy had the greatest capacity for producing and annexing dirt of any man he ever met with." Of Benjamin Woodward, the architect of the Oxford Union, he said that he was "the stillest creature that ever breathed out of an oyster-shell." On observing on one occasion two camels belonging to a menagerie shambling along through the streets, "Look," he said, "there's Ruskin and Wordsworth virtuously taking a walk." When Burne-Jones first called on Rossetti in his studio in Chatham Place, he noted that there were no books on the shelves, and Rossetti appears gravely to have said that books were no use to a painter except to prop up models upon in difficult positions, and that then they might be very useful.

The impression that remains upon the mind is that Rossetti's humour was of rather an unscrupulous kind, though on the other hand he was quick to feel remorse if he saw that pain was being given by what he said. But it cannot be too strongly insisted upon that in ordinary life he had no touch of mysterious solemnity or of artificial dignity, but rather a strong relish for humorous contrasts and witty images. He was fond of contagious jests and loud laughter, and heartily despised any attempt to view life in ordinary intercourse from any but the most natural and robust standpoint.

In early days Rossetti was decidedly indolent, not with a lethargic indolence, but with the volatile desultoriness of a man with superabundant vitality, who had a thousand schemes in his head, and who found it difficult to settle down to any one thing. His father several times took occasion to remonstrate with him very severely on his want of application, and the early letters from his friends contain lamentations that he will not set to at any definite work or finish what he has undertaken. As he grew older this insensibly altered; he grew absorbed in his work, he began to feel the pleasure of making money —indeed he spent so lavishly that money-making became a prime necessity, and his work was, as a rule, commissioned so long beforehand that he was obliged to work hard to fulfil his pledges. Moreover, his resources in the way of amusement were few; he had no physical recreations to fall back upon, as he disliked exercise; he read a good deal in an easy way, and he was fond of the society of intimate friends. Employment of some kind became a necessity to him, for to a vivid mind like Rossetti's *ennui* is the terrible foe. The result is that, considering the long periods during which his activities were suspended by illness, the amount of work he did, in poetry and painting, is very remarkable; but an interesting letter written late in life shows that he was conscious of not having at all fulfilled his destiny with respect to the work he might have done:—

"Sloth, alas! has but too much to answer for with me; and is one of the reasons (though I will not say the only one), why I have always fallen back on quality instead of quantity in the little I have ever done. I think often with Coleridge:

> 'Sloth jaundiced all : and from my graspless hand
> Drop friendship's precious pearls like hour-glass sand.
> I weep, yet stoop not : the faint anguish flows,
> A dreamy pang in morning's feverish doze.'"

The letter is a manly one, though deeply tinged with the melancholy which was characteristic of his later years.

Rossetti's attitude to practical politics was one of indifference almost amounting to aversion. He owned to taking some interest in the principles underlying the turbid surface of events, or rather he resented the imputation that he had no interest in such matters; but the life of the practical politician, the canvassing, the committees, the disagreeable preponderance of dust and din over actual results, seemed to him utterly βάναυσος and vulgar. He wrote an interesting letter on the subject in which he says:—

"I must admit, at all hazards, that my friends here consider me exceptionally averse to politics; and I suppose I must be, for I never read a Parliamentary debate in my life! At the same time I will add that, among those whose opinions I most value, some think me not altogether wrong when I venture to speak of the momentary momentousness and eternal futility of many noisiest questions. However, you must simply view me as a nonentity in any practical relation to such matters."

William Morris gave an interesting explanation of what he believed to be Rossetti's attitude of mind in these matters:—

"I can't say," he writes, "how it was that Rossetti took no interest in politics; but so it was: of course he was quite Italian in his general turn of thought; though I think he took less interest in Italian politics than in English, in spite of his knowing several of the leading patriots personally, Saffi for instance. The truth is he cared for nothing but individual and personal matters; chiefly of course in relation to art and literature, but he would take abundant trouble to help any one person who was in distress of mind or body; but the evils of any mass of people he couldn't bring his mind to bear upon. I suppose in short it needs a person of hopeful mind to take disinterested notice of politics, and Rossetti was certainly not hopeful."

A marked characteristic of Rossetti, which grew upon him in later life, was his dislike of publicity of any kind. His idea was to live his own life and dream his own dreams, and the criticism of others merely harassed and weakened him. He felt with Keats that his own criticism of his own work was far more important than the strictures of others; but he had a strong sense of his right to seclusion, and he had an almost physical sense of the humiliation of being discussed, like the character in one of Mr. Henry James's novels who says that the consciousness that he is being criticised in his absence by a man whom he dislikes, makes him feel as if the footman was wearing his hat.

In all this he was not weak, but self-willed. The mystery that grew up about his work was not of his own creating; it was rather the result of his deliberate purpose to live his life to himself, to see the friends he loved, and not to be the prey of inquisitive persons. He acted in the spirit of Ruskin's paradoxical maxim, that an artist should be fit for the best society and keep out of it. The relentless gossip which pursued him might have given a self-conscious man a pleasurable sense of importance, but it only grated on Rossetti. For there never was a man with less *pose* of any kind: he knew what his aims and desires were, and his only object was to realise these as far as possible, and in his free hours to choose such company and recreations as he desired.

It is difficult to say exactly what Rossetti's religious views were. The religious element was very strongly developed in the family, both in his mother and his two sisters; and we may infer that it was probably not absent from Rossetti himself, though appearing in a different guise. There is no evidence that he concerned himself with considerations of Christian doctrine, and he would probably have regarded theologians as people who were engaged in attempting to define the Unknowable. He was, no doubt, a free-thinker, and held an agnostic position; but at the same time he had a strong vein of superstition in his nature, and there is a good deal of evidence that in his later days his thoughts turned much on the personal relation between God and man. He desired not only forgiveness, but definite absolution, and this at a time when, though death was fast closing upon him, his intellectual force seems in no way to have lost its grip. I should regard Rossetti as having a strong belief in God and the unseen world, though without definite conceptions of what lay behind the veil, and a considerable impatience of attempts at precise definition.

It has often been questioned whether the development of the artistic nature is necessarily attended by the weakening of the moral fibre. It is so only if the artist endeavours to create for himself a fantastic seclusion, and to exclude from it the wholesome, bitter experience of life. To treat continually the tragic emotions of life as material for artistic expression is almost bound to destroy the balance of a nature, because the emotion and the tragedy are viewed, as it were, through a glass, in security, as a man may gaze on a body in the Morgue, cultivating his sensibility, without cultivating the human instinct which leads a man so far as possible to remedy and alleviate calamity.

Rossetti is generally regarded as a man who tried to create an artificial paradise, and to drown the urgent voices of the world beneath the cooing of coteries. This is an entire misconception. For the first forty years of his life he lived robustly, generously, manfully. He took his share of bright and dark, and, like the companions of Ulysses,

> "ever with a frolic welcome took
> The thunder and the sunshine, and opposed
> Free hearts, free foreheads."

He was masterful, self-willed, impatient, self-absorbed; but he was also generous of help and of sympathy, sociable, brave, enthusiastic, fond of beauty and laughter and talk. He, if any man, "warmed both hands before the fire of life."

Yet any one who carefully studies Rossetti's life and work must, I think, become gradually conscious of a certain growing disappointment as the years go on. Perhaps that is too light a word to use for a thought that carries with it a shadow of deep melancholy. The impression produced by the character and the genius of the man at his best is one of incomparable richness. Here was one of those rare spirits, full of exuberant vitality, who could produce works not only of supreme technical excellence, but works, the slightest of which betrayed a force, a vigour, a grace of extraordinary intensity, whether he wrote slowly or rapidly, whether he made a sketch, or a design, or a finished painting; everything that came from his hand had this forcible quality which we call genius, and which, whether it attracted or repelled, could not be gainsaid. His art has been well called the climax of personality; and moreover it was freely recognised by all who knew him best, that his was not a nature which had slowly made the best of and matured one species of excellence, but that his work was only a faint expression of an inner force, and streamed from him like light from the sun. Even when broken with illness and enslaved by the sad bondage of habit, this personality still dazzled and almost hypnotised all who were brought into contact with him, up to the very end.

And yet one cannot avoid the thought which is forced upon one, that he did not fulfil the possibilities of his nature. It is not ungenerous to say this, because one may at the same time gratefully admit that the body of his work is both large and of supreme excellence. But as he crosses the threshold of life he seems to be *capable de tout*. He seems the heir of the ages of art. Then, as the years go on, it is clear that the stream is contracting, and that it is being forced into smaller and smaller channels. It is not that he seems to have narrowed his output deliberately, to have recognised that to work effectively in a world of specialists it is necessary to be a specialist too. One rather feels that this opulent nature is becoming the tool of circumstance; that by deliberately excluding from his life so many wholesome human influences, the character, instead of opening freely like a flower in the free air, is growing like an exotic in the corner of a hothouse.

We would not seem to question or criticise too strictly his own power of initiative; that outer control which we name Fate or Providence does seem to have set a hedge about his spirit. His tragical marriage, his failure of health, his self-willed habits of life, all tended to isolate him unduly from the world; and the result is a lack of breadth in his work which prevents his taking the position, even in art, to which his native greatness seems to have entitled him. He is not among those who appeal to all alike; though, apart from those who are sealed of his tribe, there are many catholic-minded people with strongly balanced minds who can recognise without drawbacks the attraction of this strange, beauty-haunted dreamer; still, there will always be persons who, with a strong instinct for certain kinds of beauty, will be repelled by Rossetti's art, and feel a dim sense of uneasiness, even danger, in his conception of life; and we cannot say that this instinct is wholly wrong. This is not the moment at which to enter into the controversy which must always prevail as to whether Art can exist for its own sake without any reference to its effect on character. Possibly Art which is self-absorbed may thus reach its highest development; but the widest view would seem to be that the equable development of the whole of man's nature is the purpose which underlies the vast fabric of mortal things. If that be so, then, as Rossetti believed in his earlier days, there is a sacrifice demanded of the artist too, which is the service of man.

It was in the gnomic poem of *Soothsay* that Rossetti wrote his deliberate creed out. It may thus be summarised:—to mistrust the certainties of human knowledge, but to believe in Nature; to be independent and subservient to no man, not to nurture false hopes, but to be content to have sung truly, and to have been loved; to be consistent, to hate flattery, to be true to friendship, to be liberal, to be laborious, to abhor indolence, not to waste the golden hours; in religion to follow faith rather than dogma; to be grateful, not to waste strength in vain hope or vain regret;—so runs the symbol, based upon generosity and love, and wrought into a proud stoicism by sad experience. But though the doctrine is shadowed by melancholy, though he who framed it had learned not to expect too much from life, yet it is an essentially manly, courageous, temperate, and true creed. There is no touch of morbid sentiment here, no exotic feeling, no luxurious dalliance with emotion.

Such then was Rossetti: mystical, full of passion, haunted by the sense of beauty, with an intense need of loving and being loved; dominant, fiery, genial, robust; with a narrow outlook, and yet with a keen intellectual power; capable, generous, lavish, humorous, a natural leader of men, self-centred, unbalanced; with no touch of tranquillity about him, but eager, ardent, impatient. It is no wonder that even before his death, and during a life so strangely shadowed, so knit with tragedy, so vital and yet so doomed, he had become one of the most romantic figures of the time, and that his whole life still retains a mysterious attraction, the force of which it is impossible to gainsay or resist.

To most of us the moments of perception of the beautiful come rarely, a sudden brightness among grey hours, like blossoms springing from a ledge in a rock-face; but with Rossetti this perception appears to have been, at least in the good years of health and vigour, more or less continuous. Beauty was the atmosphere in which he lived, and to which the sordid acts of real life were but dreary interruptions.

But from the river of delight he drank too greedily. As the king in *The Sick King in Bokhara* says—

> "Thou wast a sinner, thou poor man!
> Thou wast athirst; and didst not see,
> That, though we take what we desire,
> We must not snatch it eagerly."

It is notable that, in Millais's picture of *Lorenzo and Isabella*, the portrait of Rossetti is traceable in the guest who, at the end of the long row, swallows with a curious zest and intentness of gesture the wine from his long glass—the very gesture is said to have been characteristic.

But, from the beginning of the world, this persistent care for outward beauty has brought with it weariness and satiety of spirit. And thus it was with Rossetti that his life turned to sadness. As Keats wrote of Melancholy,

"She dwells with Beauty—Beauty that must die;
   And Joy, whose hand is ever at his lips
Bidding adieu; and aching Pleasure nigh,
   Turning to poison while the bee-mouth sips:
Ay, in the very temple of Delight
   Veil'd Melancholy has her sovran shrine,
     Though seen of none save him whose strenuous tongue
   Can burst Joy's grape against his palate fine;
His soul shall taste the sadness of her might,
     And be among her cloudy trophies hung."

And so it comes to pass that the grave of Rossetti is as the tomb of Polydorus on the Thracian strand: he lay buried in a forest of spears; the very hafts of the sharp lances that had slain him had taken root, and had thrown out leaf and flower above the lonely mound; so that Æneas, when he would fain have torn a bough to deck the altars, saw the blood trickle from the broken branch, and heard in speechless horror the groans of the sad spirit rise thin upon the air. "*Jam parce sepulto*"; cried the prisoned ghost. Then in love and pity the Trojan band performed the sacred rites, laid the sorrowing spirit to rest, and sought another shore.

INDEX

A

Academy, The, 55.
Academy, The Royal, 179.
Allingham, William, 163, 164, 165, 166, 167, 173, 174, 217.
Ancient Mariner, The (Coleridge), 115, 141.
Antwerp and Bruges, 29.
Arnold, Matthew, 139.
Art of England, The (Ruskin), 183.
Astarte Syriaca (picture), 84, 186, 192.
Athenaeum, The, 24, 62, 69, 79, 162, 184.
Aurea Catena (picture), 186, 192.
Aurora Leigh (Elizabeth B. Browning), 167.
Ave, 12, 95, 98, 125-6.
Aylwin (Watts-Dunton), 61, 73, 74.

B

Ballads and Sonnets, 66.
Beata Beatrix (picture), 186, 193-4.
Before the Battle (picture), 185.
Belcolore (picture), 186, 191.
Belloc, Madame, 44.
Beryl-Songs, The, 106.
Birth-bond, The, 131.
Blake, 19, 77, 160, 161.
Blake, Life of (Gilchrist), 153, 160-2.
Blessed Damozel, The, 12, 28, 97, 113-17, 120.

Blue Closet, The (picture), 185.
Bocca Baciata (picture), 186, 191.
Boccaccio, 77.
Bonifazio's Mistress (picture), 84, 159, 181, 185.
Borgia (picture), 181, 189.
Bower Meadow, The (picture), 182.
Boyd, Miss Alice, 54.
Bride's Prelude, The, 13, 25, 66, 82, 101, 108-10.
Brown, Ford Madox, 11, 13, 14, 22, 30, 31, 42, 49, 50, 58, 81, 167, 177, 204, 206, 209, 213, 214, 217, 219.
Brown, Oliver Madox, 76, 173.
Browning, Robert, 12, 13, 64, 77, 97, 135, 139, 167, 174, 186, 196.
Buchanan, Robert, 61, 62, 63, 91, 93, 162.
Burden of Nineveh, The, 26, 89, 126-7.
Burne-Jones, 36, 37, 38, 39, 40, 42, 80, 205, 220.
Buy from us with a golden curl (picture), 195.
Byron, 139, 140.

C

Caine, Mr. Hall, 9, 58, 63, 66-70, 72, 81, 107, 165, 168, 170, 171, 172; *Recollections* of, 66, 163.
Callcott, 178.

Carillon, The, 29.
Carlyle, 166.
Carroll, Lewis, 64.
Cary, F. S., 10.
Cassandra (picture), 180, 186.
Cavalcanti, Guido, 147, 148, 149.
Chatterton, 76, 170, 173, 174.
Chaucer, 73.
Chesneau, M., 179.
Christabel (Coleridge), 141.
Christmas Carol, The (picture), 185.
Clough, Arthur, 139.
Coleridge, 76, 97, 139, 141, 169, 172, 222.
Coleridge (Cottle), 77.
Collinson, James, 22.
Commedia, Divina (Dante), 147.
Coriolanus (Shakespeare), 169.
Cornelius (painter), 18.
Correggio, 160.
Cowper, 165.
Crashaw, 98.

D

Dante, 7, 8, 12, 77, 147, 151, 152.
Dante at Verona, 13, 25, 82, 121-2.
Dante drawing the Angel (picture), 180.
Dante's Dream (picture), 180, 188-9.
Day and Night Songs (W. Allingham), 194.
Day-Dream, The (picture), 186.
Delaroche, 183.
Deverell, W. H., 44, 45.
Dickens, 77.
Dixon, Canon, 111.
"Dizzy" (dog), 165, 168.
Dobell, Sydney, 82, 170.
Donne, 77.
Dumas, 77.
Dyce, 179.

E

Early Italian Poets, 8, 48, 195.
Ecce Ancilla Domini (picture), 24, 185, 187.
Eden Bower, 93, 101, 112.
Enzo, King, 150.
Even So, 81.
Eve of St. Agnes, The (Holman Hunt's picture), 14.
Eve of St. Agnes, The (Keats), 99.
Eve of St. Mark, The (Keats), 99.

F

Fazio's Mistress, see *Bonifazio*.
Fiammetta (picture), 186, 191.
Fifine at the Fair (Browning), 64.
Flandrin (painter), 177.
Fleshly School of Poetry, The (Buchanan), 61, 94, 162-3.
Fortnightly Review, The, 56.
Found (picture), 25, 117, 185, 187, 190-1, 204.
Fra Pace (picture), 187-8.
From the Cliffs, 29.
Fuseli, 178.

G

Gainsborough, 178.
Gate of Memory, The (picture), 186.
Germ, The, 27-30, 116, 158.
Gesta Romanorum, 111.
Gilchrist, Alexander, 153, 160.
Giotto, 20.
Girlhood of Mary Virgin, The (picture), 15, 23, 185.
Goblin Market (Christina Rossetti), 194.
Gosse, Mr., 41, 107, 169, 208.

H

Hamlet and Ophelia (picture), 181, 185, 189-90.
Hand and Soul, 28, 30, 153-8.
Haydon, 178.

INDEX 233

Hiawatha (Longfellow), 173.
Hill, Dr. Birkbeck, 163, 217.
Hill Summit, The, 88.
Hireling Shepherd, The (Holman Hunt's picture), 25.
Hist! said Kate the Queen (picture), 180.
Hogarth, 19, 182, 183.
Houghton, Lord, 19.
House of Life, The, 66, 79, 84, 85, 129-37, 176.
How shall I your true love know? 88.
How they met Themselves (picture), 47, 185.
Hughes, Arthur, 42, 215.
Hunt, Mr. Holman, 12, 14, 15, 21, 22, 23, 24, 30, 45, 178, 187, 196, 217, 220.
Hunt, Leigh, 15.
Hunting of the Snark, The (Lewis Carroll), 64.

I

Ingres (painter), 177, 186.
Insomnia, 128.

J

James, Mr. Henry, 224.
Jan Van Hunks, 72.
Jenny, 13, 25, 26, 117-21.
Johnson, Dr., 168, 169.
Johnson (Boswell), 68, 77.
Johnson at the Mitre, Dr. (picture), 184, 185, 190.

K

Keats, 12, 73, 76, 80, 85, 99, 135, 139, 141, 170, 171, 172, 176, 223, 230.
Keats, Life and Letters of (Lord Houghton), 19.

Keith of Ravelston (Sydney Dobell), 170.
Kelmscott, 41, 59, 60, 64, 96.
King Arthur's Tomb (picture), 185.
King's Quhair, The (James I.), 108.
King's Tragedy, The, 66, 74, 101, 107-8.

L

La Bella Mano (picture), 192.
La Belle Dame Sans Merci (Keats), 170, 171.
Laboratory, The (picture), 185.
Lady of Shalott, The (Tennyson), 98, 194.
Lady with the Fan, The (picture), 192.
Landseer, 179.
La Pia (picture), 186.
Last Confession, A, 13, 26, 97, 123-4.
Lawrence, Sir Thomas, 178.
Leaves of Grass (Walt Whitman), 173.
Lee, Frederic (painter), 178.
Leonardo da Vinci, 16, 20.
Leslie, 19.
Letters and Memoirs (W. M. Rossetti), 163.
Letters, Rossetti's, 163 seq.
Lilith (picture), 186, 192.
Livy, 142.
Longfellow, 173.
Lorenzo and Isabella (Millais's picture), 229.
Lost Days, 133.
Love Enthroned, 130.
Love-Lily, 129.
Love's Nocturn, 90, 91.
Love-Sweetness, 131.
Loving Cup, The (picture), 186, 191.
Lucrezia Borgia (picture), 185.

Lyell, Sir Charles, 3.
Lyell, Mr. Charles, 3.
Lytton, Lord, 143.

M

Mackail, Mr., 39, 203.
Madness of Ophelia, The (picture), 185.
Marochetti (sculptor), 180.
Marston, Philip Bourke, 41, 207.
Mary Magdalen at the Door of Simon (picture), 180.
Mary's Girlhood, 137, 138.
Match with the Moon, A, 89.
Maurice, F. D., 35.
Mazzini, 7.
McCracken, Mr. (art patron), 31, 165, 182.
Meinhold, Wilhelm, 174.
Memling, 177.
Men and Women (Browning), 37.
Merciless Lady, The (picture), 181, 185, 189.
Meredith, Mr. George, 51.
Millais, John Everett, 14, 15, 16, 20, 22, 23, 24, 45, 159, 180, 187, 229.
Milton, 62, 77, 135, 168.
More, Hannah, 168.
Morland, 178.
Morris, William, 36, 37, 38, 39, 40, 41, 55, 75, 76, 82, 176, 196, 205, 206, 210, 218, 220, 223.
Morris, William, Life of (Mackail), 39.
Morte d'Arthur (Malory), 39.
Mulready, 19.
Murray, Mr. Fairfax, 41, 91.
Myers, Frederic, 197.
My Sister's Sleep, 28, 94.

N

Nasmyth, 178.
Nibelungenlied, 12.
Nineteenth Century, 80.

O

On the Field of Waterloo, 87.
One Hope, The, 88.
Ophelia (Millais's picture), 25.
O'Shaughnessy, Arthur, 41.
Oxford, 36, 37, 39.
Oxford and Cambridge Magazine, 111, 116, 126.
Overbeck, 18.

P

Paganini, 7.
Painting, English school of, 19, 20, 178-80; French, 177, 178; Italian, 177; Belgian, 177; Dutch, 177.
Palace of Art, The (picture), 194.
Pandora, 138; (picture), 186, 193.
Panizzi, 7.
Paolo and Francesca (picture), 181, 185.
Pater, Walter, 41, 82, 107, 142, 151.
Patmore, Coventry, 25, 28, 81, 143.
Paton, Noël, 179.
Pauline (Browning), 13.
Poe, E. A., 77.
Poetry of nineteenth century, 78, 139 *seq.*
Polidori, Gaetano, 4, 8, 175.
—— Frances Mary Lavinia, 4.
Portrait, The, 84, 91, 95, 98, 124-5.
Præterita (Ruskin), 35, 202.
Pre-Raphaelites, The, 18 *seq.*, 99, 178, 179, 217, 219.
Prince's Progress, The (Christina Rossetti), 194.
Proserpine (picture), 186, 193.
Punch, 216.

R

Raeburn, 178.
Recollections of Rossetti (Hall Caine), 66, 163.

Regina Cordium (picture), 186.
Rembrandt, 160.
Retro me, Sathana! 88.
Return of Tibullus, The (picture), 193.
Reynolds, Sir Joshua, 20, 160, 178.
Romney, 178.
Rose Mary, 66, 74, 91, 92, 93, 101, 102, 104-7.
Rossetti, Gabriel Charles Dante: birth and family history, 3; literary tastes as a boy, 7, 8; first efforts at writing, 8; school, 9; disposition as a boy, 9, 10, 12; enters drawing academy, 10; great intellectual activity as a youth, 12, 13; translates Dante's *Vita Nuova*, 12; writes *The Blessed Damozel, Ave, Dante at Verona, The Bride's Prelude, A Last Confession, Jenny*, 12, 13; pupil of Madox Brown, 14; friendship with Holman Hunt and Millais, 14, 16; shares studio with Holman Hunt, 15; first important picture, 15, 23; hesitates between painting and literature, 15, 80, 81; effect of early surroundings on his work, 16; a founder of the Pre-Raphaelite Brotherhood, 18 *seq.*; wide acquaintance with poetical literature generally, 22; methods of work as a painter, 23; exhibits *The Girlhood of Mary Virgin* and *Ecce Ancilla Domini*, 24; attacked by the *Times* and *Athenaeum*, 24; defended by Ruskin, 25; designs his great picture *Found*, 25; turns again to poetry, 25; *Sister Helen* and other poems, 25-6; desultory habits, 26; abandons poetry temporarily, 26; publication of the *Germ*, 27; hard times, 31; friendship with Ruskin, 31; Ruskin's generosity, 31; Ruskin's letters to him, 32-3; helps Maurice at the Working Men's College, 35; visits Oxford, 36; relations with Burne-Jones and William Morris, 36 *seq.*; friendship with younger men of promise, 41; partnership with William Morris, 41; strained relations, 42, 43; falls in love, 45; marriage, 47; publishes *Early Italian Poets*, 48; mode of life, 48, 52, 60; death of his wife, 49; buries MS. of unpublished poems with her, 50; moves to Tudor House, Chelsea, 51; narrow views of art and literature, 51; artistic and financial success, 53; goes abroad, 53; physical trouble, 53; income, 53, 203; recovery of poems from his wife's grave, 55; their publication and triumphant reception, 55, 56; use of chloral, 57, 64, 66, 69; lives at Kelmscott with William Morris 59; friendship with Mr. Watts-Dunton, 61; attacked by Buchanan in the *Contemporary Review*, 61; mind becomes unhinged, 64; delusions, 64-5; illness, 64, 65; friendship with Mr. Hall Caine, 66; new edition of the *Poems*, 66; *Ballads and Sonnets*, 66; wanderings in search of health, 64, 65, 71; returns to Cheyne Walk, 71; increasing illness and depression, 71; death at Birchington, 72; method of composition, 74; a great reader, 75; favourite authors, 76-7; characteristics of his poetry, 78 *seq.*; his message, 79-80; theory of writing, 81; sense of beauty, 83; two distinct manners, 83; melancholy of his poems, 84; use of words, 84;

ROSSETTI

sonnets, 29, 85-9, 129-38; lyrics, 86, 87, 127-9; humour and fantasy, 89; music of his verse, 90; use of the supernatural, 90; artistic restraint, 89, 90, 96, 97; intensity, 92; rhymes, 93, 94; parody of his style by Buchanan, 94; simplicity of his early poems, 94-5; essentially an indoors poet, 95; influence of other poets on him, 97; development of and alterations in his poems, 29-30, 91, 102, 115-16; influence on English poetry, 142-4; position in relation to the literature of the century, 139 *seq.*; translations, 145 *seq.*; soundness of his criticism, 148, 161, 162, 169-75; his Italian models, 146 *seq.*; prose writings, 152, 162; gift for letter-writing, 163 *seq.*; voluptuousness of his poetry, 62, 63, 135, 136; his painting, 176 *seq.*; Ruskin's estimate of him, 176, 177; chief artistic influences, 177 *seq.*; Madox Brown's great influence on him, 177-80; technical limitations, 180, 181, 187; originator of a new type of female beauty, 181; primarily a colourist, 182; his colour preferences, 182; watercolours, 182-4; methods and mannerisms, 184-5, 199; models, 185; various classes of pictures, 185-6; mediæval, 186; Dante series, 188-90; dramatic, 189-90; genre pictures, 190-1; half-length female figures, 191-4; book illustrations, 194-5; nature and aim of his art, 195 *seq.*; character and description, 202 *seq.*; lack of sympathy, 35; intellectual dominance, 34, 36, 37, 39, 40, 195-6, 203, 204, 206, 226; eloquence, 40, 70; charm of manner, 40, 206, 218; collector of *bric-à-brac* and queer animals, 52; his moral side, 56; an Italian by instinct, 62, 78, 202; beauty of his voice, 67, 70; religious views, 71, 224-5; portraits of him, 73, 229; personal appearance and characteristics, 11, 67, 72, 73, 208; passion for beauty, 202; susceptibility to feminine charm, 202; devotion to his mother, 168, 211-12; generous appreciation of the work of others, 208-10; greatness as a man, 203; acuteness and penetration, 203; keenness in money matters, 204, 215; friendships, 206-7; generosity, 215; naturalness, 216, 219, 224; fondness for slang, 217; unconventionality, 218; humour, 219-21; dislike of publicity, 223; many good qualities, 205, 213, 215, 225; faults, 204, 205, 210; philosophic creed, 130, 228; summing up, 229-30.

Rossetti, Gabriele (father), 3, 4, 5, 7, 8, 9, 10, 26, 212.

—— Mrs., *née* Polidori (mother), 3, 4, 5, 6, 26, 72, 74, 168, 186, 211-13.

—— Nicola (grandfather), 4.

—— Maria Francesca (sister), 6.

—— William Michael (brother), 6, 13, 22, 23, 27, 42, 51, 91, 108, 163, 207, 212, 215.

—— Christina (sister), 6, 28, 72, 74, 88, 135, 142, 143, 186, 194.

—— Mrs., *née* Siddal (wife), 25, 34, 44-51, 215.

Rubens, 160.

Ruskin, 16, 25, 31-5, 36, 46, 47, 48, 126, 176, 179, 180, 183, 202, 205, 206, 220, 224.

S

Saint Agnes of Intercession, 9, 17, 153, 158-60.
Salutation of Beatrice, The (picture), 180.
Scott, Sir Walter, 139, 140.
—— W. Bell, 35, 46, 54, 166.
Sea-Spell, The (picture), 192.
Shakespeare, 62, 76, 135, 170.
Sharp, Mr. William, 117.
Shelley, 12, 76, 139, 140, 171, 172.
Shelley (Hogg), 77.
Sick King in Bokhara, The, 229.
Siddal, Miss. *See* Rossetti, Mrs.
Sidonia the Sorceress (Meinhold), 174.
Sigurd the Volsung (William Morris), 75.
Sir Galahad (picture), 185.
Sir Hugh the Heron, 8.
Sir Lancelot's Vision of the Sangrail (fresco), 36.
Sir Tristram and La Belle Yseult (picture), 184.
Sister Helen, 92, 97, 101-4.
Sleepless Dreams, 87.
Smetham, James, 186.
Soothsay, 228.
Sorrentino, 12.
Soul's Beauty, 131.
Sphinx, The (picture), 186.
Spring, 137, 138.
Staff and Scrip, The, 86, 92, 101, 110-12.
Stanfield (painter), 178.
Stanley, Dean, 218.
Stealthy School of Criticism, The, 62.
Stephens, F. G. (art critic), 22.
Stevenson, R. L., 142.
Stratton Water, 98, 101, 113.
Stream's Secret, The, 54, 80, 127-8.
Superscription, A, 87.
Swedenborg, 77.

Swinburne, 41, 46, 51, 56, 142, 143, 186, 205.

T

Tennyson, 12, 75, 96, 124, 139, 140, 142, 143, 176.
Tennyson-Turner, 77.
Times, The, 24, 209.
Titian, 160, 182.
Tommaseo, Niccolò, 150.
Toussaint L'Ouverture (Wordsworth), 175.
Troy Town, 101, 112.
Tupper, J. L., 28, 29.
Turner, 32, 178.

U

Union, The Oxford, Frescoes of, 36, 37.

V

Van Eyck, 177.
Venetian Pastoral, A, 29, 137.
Venus Verticordia, 138, 192.
Veronica Veronese (picture), 186, 192.
Vita Nuova, translation of Dante's, 12, 145, 147, 151-2.

W

Ward's English Poets, 82.
Washing Hands (picture), 185.
Water Willow (picture), 59.
Watts-Dunton, Mr., 61, 69, 72, 76, 80, 106, 180, 181.
Wedding of St. George, The (picture), 186.
West, Benjamin, 178.
Whistler, 178.
Whitman, Walt, 173.
White Ship, The, 66, 70, 101, 107, 108.
Wilkie, 19, 183.

Willow-wood, 162.
Winter, 137, 138.
Without Her, 132-3.
Woods of Westermain, The, 200.
Woodward, Benjamin (architect), 36, 220.
Woolner (sculptor), 22, 28, 166, 219.

Wordsworth, 77, 139, 140, 174, 175, 197, 220.
Working Men's College, Ormond Street, 35, 49.
World is too much with us, The (Wordsworth), 175.
Wuthering Heights (Emily Brontè), 174.

Lightning Source UK Ltd.
Milton Keynes UK
17 January 2011

165872UK00001B/9/A